ON MY WAY
BEYOND THE HOUSE OF FIVE SENSES

SUMMER INTERN EXPERIENCES AT
GROWING WHEEL INTERNATIONAL

SUSAN GURNEE, DIRECTOR
ASSISTED BY INÉE ADER

Also Available:

Chain of Diamonds A Gardening Book of Self-Discovery

Intuition Enhancement (available in soft cover in English and German from *www.amazon.com*.)

Vitality, Stamina and Endurance (available as an e-book in German and English)

Pessomancy – Future-telling with stones (available as an e-book in German and English)

Diamond Gardening (available as an e-book in German, Spanish and English)

Muscle Response Testing (available as an e-book in German and English)

Sue Gurnee, Autobiography of a Healer

Mutuality Handbook (available as an e-book in German and English)

Platforms of Evolution (available as an e-book in English)

AuthorHouse ™
1663 Liberty Drive
Bloomington, IN 47403
www.authorhouse.com

ISBN: 978-1-4772-7034-9 (sc)
ISBN: 978-1-4772-7035-6 (e)
Library of Congress Control Number: 2012917113

Dedicated to the participants who enrich
this program each year with
their contributions.

TABLE OF CONTENTS

PREFACE

On these pages you will vicariously spend the summer in Todd, North Carolina. The book has many voices — from volunteers past and present who have changed their lives while falling in love. The love they found was always there. Inside. In Todd, this love was nurtured. It found its presence through powers of newfound courage, communication and the trust that each soul is graced with inner wisdom.

No matter what time of year you find yourself reading these lovers' words, you will feel the essence of the adventures that happen inside and beyond the House of Five Senses. You will meet Inée through her journal writings. You will read insights from alumni volunteers who range in age from 20 to 60+. If you care to study with them, there are lesson summations sprinkled across the chapters. These lessons, sewn together by Sue Gurnee are tailored to fit the myriad of activities that crop up during the summers. The chapters of the book are compiled from timeless teachings designed for culturally diverse and strong-minded questers. Like a gentle migration, each year indomitable searchers make their way to the hidden higher-purpose haven called Growing Wheel. Then as the leaves ripen to red, with trusted new friends they wing away and share their perceptions with others. The fruits for the organization are memories, sweet and fresh.

When you read the mosaic of love-learned passages you will notice that some lessons are drafted in first person and others in third person reflecting the past. It seemed tender to keep these as inscribed, for it mimics the fluidity of the mind as it wanders from the past to future. To the reader it is hoped that this will be as natural as the setting here - far away from the constraints of conventional style. It is assumed that most who wander these pages are technology-acquainted so the versatility gained from texting, tweeting, reading prose, poetry and classical texts is sufficient to follow our ways. Many interns claim English as their second or third language. These brilliant assimilators continue to remind us that communication is not syntax-bound.

Settle into a comfortable chair. Relax. (If you are an editor by profession — put down your red pen. Engage from the feeling level.) Join us by rocking back and forth between the ideas, the perceptions, and the myriad of discoveries bridged to words plucked from the invisible realm of energetics and translated to you.

Sue Gurnee
August 14, 2012
House of Five Senses
Todd, North Carolina
USA

INTRODUCTION
GROWING WHEEL INTERN PROGRAM

The role of an intern is a multi-disciplinary one. Filled by self-directed men and women, for the past 18 years volunteers from various parts of the globe have taken the inner challenge to learn about themselves while engaged in household and farming tasks that center the mind and enhance the senses.

Growing Wheel International is not a summer camp in any ordinary sense. It is a non-profit and tax-exempt educational organization that opens its gates each year to individuals interested in including the power of energetics into their lives. This organization offers its highly acclaimed summer opportunity to those who speak English and are in excellent health. The experience of an intern skillfully fuses universal concepts into practical life activities. During their service period in the hills of Todd, participants gain new perspectives about autonomy. While engaged in summer routines they widen their perceptions and forge the truths that emerge beyond logical thought. The effects of thoughts, actions, speech, and energy transference are woven into lessons each day.

The program's structure is juxtaposed against a rugged setting at the end of a narrow dirt road. Its theme has attracted luminaries and politicians, CEO's and celebrities, to what seems at first glance, like an unpredictable and unlikely compound of architecturally idiosyncratic structures. Hours worth of hiking trails are scattered over more than a hundred acres of pastures and forestland. All the food served from any of the five kitchens is lovingly grown and carefully prepared here. It is in an iconoclastic setting that interns study the energetic alliances that occur during interactions with people, animals, and the environment.

There is no traditional committee that interviews applicants. Qualified applicants send a letter of introduction. Using a graph of potentials, each hopeful is examined at distance. Those who have the distinguishing qualities to explore and grow are accepted. Once involved, they take full responsibility for their actions. They are treated as fellow colleagues to the mission. Comfortable cabins are provided and food is often shared in community in the many indoor and outdoor dining areas.

Director Sue Gurnee explains that since the inception of the program, which seemed to just happen ("...by chance", she says with a smile) scores of extremely talented and spiritually-minded interns have made their way here. There are no grades, diplomas, or prizes given to any intern after his summer study at Growing Wheel. An intern's reward is the assimilation of information that widens the panorama of enjoyments and fulfillments. Many who have benefited from the program have become benefactors of the non-profit organization. Special thanks to all alumni who have continued to support the Intern Program as it continues the mission of the organization.

Sue explains:

After perusing the Growing Wheel website, people call me to ask further about summer experience. This book is a response to that curiosity. Many times I have formulated sentences with points that explain the program this way:

"Like-minded people from Kenya to Kentucky, Italy to Iran have challenged themselves to become "empty" and then refilled by:

• Extracting meaning from perceptions and sensations
• Objectively reassessing subtle causes and their effects using kinesiology
• Reconfiguring personally constructed inner territory to align with outer reality
• Gaining clear boundaries within his own personal code of ethics
• Attaining authentic self-confidence
• Maintaining a flexible and strong social identity that reflects courage, love, and wisdom

If this waterfall of explanations does not overwhelm them, I know they have the inner fortitude to pursue our mission and perhaps join us at a future date. We work and play here with a great satisfaction in all we do. Read on and we shall share more.

CHAPTER ONE

THE LAND AND ITS ENERGIES
GROWING WHEEL PROPERTY

Growing Wheel's equalizing energies are a common topic among visitors. With the reminder that energies are in everything and that even a person's personal energies will be affected here, I carefully explain that many changes can take place while spending time at this location.

I have high sense perception and work daily with energies that I can see at hand or at distance. Growing Wheel has attracted many talented students from around the globe interested in strengthening their innate gifts of healing. "As a research facility, this location was chosen ('...by chance', Sue smilingly remarks as a refrain). I would not have had the opportunity to do such in-depth research had it not been for a few synchronistic events early in the 1990's. I often send waves of gratitude to those who brought me to this place. I send these waves again now."

THE LAND AND ITS ENERGIES

In 1994 the previous owner found that she was disturbed by the energetics left on the land from past inhabitants. Sue Gurnee was hired, as she was known to have extraordinary skills to reconfigure the vibrational disturbances on the land.

The rough and staunch pioneers of the early 1800's made their way from Europe to a bleak and forbidding homestead site. They had to remain resourceful to survive. They built a log home adjacent to a natural spring's resurgence in a beautiful rock-strewn sinkhole called the Hidden Valley. They raised cattle and their families with a focus on the instructions of the Bible. For more than a hundred years their beliefs overlaid on the energies of the landscape.

"Seeing energies as I do, I assumed that this re-patterning would not take very long to complete. Just like the renovation of an old farmhouse, for example, after I began working I found that the layers that needed repair energetically became more and more complex. Once I was involved in the systematic work, I admitted that past experiences were not adequate to estimate the complexity of the discord that existed after settlers claimed the virginal wooded ecosystem. I had certainly miscalculated the intensity of my future involvement when I nodded my head and agreed to help her. I could spend the rest of the chapters recounting the strange and unexplainable occurrences I withstood while living alone and doggedly completing the tasks that I said I would accomplish in these hills. What a wonderful training ground it became."

Sue spent seven years as the full-time caretaker and energy balancer. One Friday in a surprise call, when the owner announced she wanted to sell the property, Sue bought it.

She continued her energy explorations. These investigations became an enveloping passion. Her quest was to renew the acreage to its most stable state. From there her goal was to create a hundred-acre landform Tree of Life encircled with 22 paths of energetic virtues. She believed that this ancient configuration on the landscape would bring awakenings to all those attracted to the power spot that fosters growth and development.

"I maintained a seasonal bio-inventory of three acres of the land and used these positive findings to verify the physical changes that accompanied my energy experiments. I worked with the property's water sources and used the central pond as a homeopathic-type energizer to transfer energy to other water features at distance. I became proficient at sending hundreds of distinctive balancing vibrations to other locations. Strict with myself to consistently remain objective, I learned to detach from the many extraordinary healing achievements that occurred using the energy transfer methods I devised.

"In 2000 I felt I had completed my apprenticeship as an energy worker and moved to the stage of journeyman by taking my skills to the next step. With the earmarked savings I accumulated, I employed two extremely talented and sensitive heavy equipment operators (they do exist), to help me with a plan. This, I thought, would complete the finishing steps of my long-term land-balancing scheme. With the expertise and knowledge to keep the land from eroding, we finally laid out the physical paths of the Kabbalah landform that stretched across the mountainous hundred acres. Trees were carefully cut up and used for firewood. Deer trails were incorporated to follow the best use of the terrain. It was a balancing act to keep the forest calm while being disturbed by the machine's sounds, and I used my energetic communication skills to quiet the animals and plants that were frightened. I had to make hard decisions about my quest and its impact on the ecosystem around me. Each night I worked to minimize the energetic discord as the path work progressed. This was a complicated undertaking.

"It was ten years from the day that the equipment first began realizing the plan that I announced that I had reached my intended objective. It had begun with a simple premise: if God is everywhere, He also lies in mental, spiritual or emotional pleasures and pains. By incorporating eternal traditions with Universal Principles, evolutionary and noble qualities align. I knew I had accomplished my endeavor when I walked the completed trails for the first time."

Sue wrote:

I asked a student from Texas who was a bodybuilder and familiar with the power of energetics if he would help me with a most important step -- that of integrating the Kabbalah energies with the landform. After deliberation, he said he was ready and we walked up the side pillar paths. He took the masculine side pillar and I walked from the south to the north on the parallel feminine pillar. Then, at a time we previously agreed, we planned to meet at Keter and thus join these paths. He walked northwest, and I northeast, and we met at the rocky mountain outcropping. What occurred after we united the paths is hard to recount. At Keter we both felt exalted and peace-filled. We did not speak and did not look at each other.

We walked together from Keter-crown back down the mountain on the Central Pillar into the Central Pillar room I built in my home. My heart raced as we entered the house. We sat in rattan chairs and a multileveled process began. He was surging with energy. All at once his head was forced back as if he was in a wind tunnel. He held on tightly to the seat's arms. His face was stretched. I endeavored to remain fluid. As for me it felt like I was water skiing through elemental and historic waters. I did not want to close my eyes. I did not want to keep them open. I let my jaw drop and focused on him. His face was red and his eyes were squinting. Minutes passed before we could move. Like any act of nature, after the energetic whirlwind subsided, we were able to stand straight up. It was not wind. It was force. We experienced what I am able to describe as strength of being. The birds had been quiet during this time. We said nothing to each other. Motioning to the jeep, he jumped into the driver's seat and we drove off the property to spend a few hours away from the land while the process completed. We felt humbled, and physically spent. After returning we tried to talk about what happened but it was not possible. I write here only a pinch of the experience shared by the wondrousness of nature.

Over the years, when people ask which of the paths of the Tree would be the best for them to walk, I take out an old deck of cards, that was made by a Kabbalah-lover named Bob. "Place yourself on the Tree", I say and I then give them my well-worn deck. After they tune-in and choose a card from my Kabbalah deck, they walk the mountainous terrain to have their special experience. Divination cards are not separate from you. They in themselves do not have an answer. Everything has a vibration.

THE LAND AND ITS ENERGIES

Divination cards and their distinctive and well-tuned frequencies resonate with your personal vibration of inquiry. It is a shame that few people remember the resources they have at their fingertips to make use daily of a seemingly innocent deck of playing cards. Students have benefitted from divination techniques as an entry point to many new beginnings.

One intern wrote:

The time I've spent in the Kabbalah wood was one of the most intense and revealing encounters with nature I've had by now. The first moments merely seemed to be a beautiful spot of land, but turned out to be a dialogue with nature on levels beyond words. It is a very kind wood, that walking along with respect and mindfulness shows you the path that is just right for the moment; indicating with light, shadow, branches, creatures, et cetera, where to step.

Trusting on every step, it carries you on profound energies and can be felt, changing with the different areas. Emotions got unblocked and resolved by lifting branches or learning how to move along effortlessly on a more challenging path. The wood has got humor as well and can give advice by unexpected sights, or seemingly dead ends that open at the last second.

Opening to the nature, a deep cleansing process and alignment of inner energies took place that have not been lead by logic or will. There is no reason to be worried there, as the wood will just resonate to your own needs. After my way through the Kabbalah, it felt like weight and junk had been taken away and fertilized. Confidence in my own steps has been risen, plus it was fun. Walk it with humbleness and the trees will applaud you.

CHAPTER TWO

MANY MEMORIES
TO SHARE

Volunteers who have helped maintain the trails over the years have their special stories to tell. Some are metaphysical, others physical. Our place is not a utopia. There are times when a roof will leak or a truck can get stuck in a ditch. When we know we must care for happenings on the manifested level in uncomfortable situations we sing out.

"Attitude Matters. Energies are powerful. Each person is powerful."

It is with a creative outlook that we assemble for all varieties of efforts and share our creative solutions. Yes, attitude does matter.

What is different about our cultivated lifestyle? The only thing I can say for sure is that we strive to utilize an unpretentious philosophy. It sounds basic. We use principled consciousness in all we do. This is the delicate balance of the masculine – action principle to do or make things while savoring the feminine aspect of experiencing our five senses and the responses that emerge at every step. We use muscle-response testing to sharpen our inner knowing. We attend to our emotions. We carefully feed and nurture our physical and emotional bodies, and become aware of the energetics of interactions. The rest naturally follows as shared powers of love.

One intern recounts:

This wild and totally natural place in the Appalachian Mountains is unusual. Every walkway stone on the property was chosen through a process called dowsing – I like this term better than muscle testing. With the help of only one other, I moved more than 2 tons of stones where dowsing showed me to place them. It took two of us less than a day to move more than 100 oversized granite step stones into a perfect arrangement. Growing Wheel is the only place I have ever been where all the decisions – like the placement of buildings, the shape and design of gazebos, color and contents of all things on the property were chosen through dowsing. It is really a cool place. This convinced me. I use dowsing every day now. Dowsing is a folk term for a process of kinesiological muscle-response testing. This uses the body as a tuning fork to resonate with information from beyond the reaches of logic.

For those who are not familiar with muscle-response testing there is a special section in this book to use if you want to learn.

CHAPTER THREE

THE HOUSE OF
FIVE SENSES

The House of Five Senses, located in the center of Growing Wheel's property on one of the Kabbalah paths (Divine Action) is a formed concrete and stucco building decorated with leaded glass windows, a slate roof and mosaic decorations constructed in 2005 by volunteers who took the challenge to build a structure using information gained through muscle-response testing.

The intention was devised by a group who took interest in experimenting with the use of principled consciousness to take a complex project to completion. Reminded daily that principled consciousness is a mindfulness that uses the balance of the reflexive and participatory aspects of cognizance, the project seemed audacious.

Before embarking, they wrote out their vision statement for this gathering place on the property.

It read:

The House of Five Senses—a sacred space for meeting and for eating, for communing and for respecting the bounties of nature

In this four-season structure people convene to:

- Refine their sensory awarenesses
- Elevate their appreciation of the wondrous aspects of the natural world
- Congregate with children above the age of 10 and
- Create a backdrop that supports the miracle of being.

It has to be:

- Handicapped accessible
- Low maintenance
- Wood floored for animals and people
- Filled with light
- Fitted into the landscape and
- Easily built by beginners engaged in the principled consciousness project

With the aid of professionals and novices, the structure was completed in less than a year. It continues to be the heart of the summer intern's activities.

"Tell the story about the stained glass window, please!" called out one of the helpers.

"Just about the time we were closing in the second floor I awoke with a heavy-headed feeling that made me check what kind of dream I had. It certainly was not a restful or rejuvenating type of sleep. It was not the feeling from residue related to energetic interference. This was a dream that had information for the betterment of all. I felt I had been in a musty basement. My head felt like it was full of mold and dust. I wrote down the major points of the dream. There was something important I was to do with the information I received. After lunch I started on a hunt.

"My dream notes read:

Odd Fellows, Asheville. Seven wooden doors leaning up against a tall and dark warehouse wall with clerestory windows. The number 800 – visible over the entire scene.

800. A toll free number? No, I was sure I should just call Information in Asheville.

'What listing in Asheville', said the operator flatly.

'What business? Ah. Odd Fellows.'

'Wait, one moment for the number.' I jotted it down with the area code, took a breath and was ready for the next step. While dialing the number I prepared my speech.

'Odd Fellows, Alison speaking.'

'Hi. I believe you have a special window there that I think is behind some doors in the back of your warehouse.'

'Yes,' She said, 'the stained glass framed pieces. They are from England.'

'Do you know how much they cost?' I asked her.

'I haven't looked at their price recently. They have been here a while. Here is the ticket. Yes. There are three panels. Each one is $2,400.'

'What is the subject matter? Do you know?'

And she said 'It has been a while since I looked at them. I think horses.'

"My mind started swimming. After a few moments of smelling the distant mustiness, the window's images began to formulate. Sandwiched against each other the shapes were difficult to read. I could feel over the phone that many pieces were broken. I saw an arch and noted that half of the first panel contained shades of blue but the other two confused me and one image seemed doubled.

'Are the windows in good shape?' I asked her.

'Some pieces are broken.'

'Ah. Would you ask your boss if he would take $800 for all three?'

"Within minutes Alison returned my call. The windows had been there for quite a while and a new shipment of antiques was due to arrive any day. The windows were mine if I wanted them. I felt a surge of persuasion in my heart and added, 'That includes delivery doesn't it?' "

I still laugh when I remember how the windows were freely delivered to my site manager's next door neighbor. Her full time occupation happened to be church window restoration. She estimated that the windows were from the 1880's and were probably the feature above a bar in a pub. The subject matter was simple and lovely. The left and right panels are mirror images of a horse being led by a pilgrim on a road that converged in the central panel at an arched bridge above a river.

After the glass artist repaired the fourteen cracked pieces, then Matthew loaded them into the bed of his pickup truck for the installation. The west wall of the second floor of the House of Five Senses now contains a 15' wide and 4' high leaded glass window triptych. It fits perfectly into the open space that remained a gaping hole until I had a dream.

CHAPTER FOUR

THE FOUR APPROACHES

Each intern displays a distinctive style of assimilating new experiences. Over time I devised this method to place people from diverse backgrounds into groups for projects, so together all could achieve optimal success.

This system loosely corresponds to the Native American tradition of the Four Directions.

Observation is a great skill to acquire. Here is a recounting of an assembly of newcomers to Growing Wheel.

One intern actively listens, and then arranges his notes in legibly scripted penmanship in a carefully organized 3-ring notebook. The notebook's cover is encased in plastic to guard against weather mishaps. There is a folder in the notebook for handouts and a zippered clear plastic place for colored pens.

One wildly enthusiastic intern moves noisily into the group knocking into chairs while making her way to an empty seat with a collection of things bundled in her arms. Aside from an over-the-shoulder handbag, an extra long-sleeved shirt and an inside-out sweater; she carries a water bottle and a pair of flip flops hooked to her index finger. She interrupts and tosses out personal stories, seems jolly and shares her enthusiasm. She writes in a small gold and maroon decoratively covered blank journal. Her pen is purple and it has a taped turkey feather around the end. She does not like to sit in one place for very long and is often distracted by the birdcalls around the property. Before the rest of the group can come to a consensus, she has full comprehension of the steps understood from envisioning the larger picture. She interrupts the slow talkers and often is misunderstood as she tries to help.

One buoyant and trendy intern makes sure the newly met buddies are assembled before she sits down with them. This intern gathers information about where each person is staying on the campus, and quickly learns their relational statuses. By engaging in off-handed conversations she learns about each one's general well-being.

One quiet student seems not to be listening but he achieves a high comprehension of the material. When the lesson is completed, in a well-structured manner he recounts the major points and then segues to his question in order to continue refining the facts he obtained in the training. He speaks only if asked direct questions and knows the names of all the interns after first introductions.

Each of these students grasps the information presented. Each incorporates the subject matter from a different vantage point. Each approaches new experiences from one of four directions.

One summer evening when the brick pizza oven in the House of Five Senses was fired up, these four volunteers entered into a group activity. Within minutes of placing the ingredients on the granite kneading board, I observed how four people, who did not know each other well, used their distinctive approaches to band together and create a delicious meal. Each continued to use his or her distinctive approach when engaged in a group activity. In the context of measuring, mixing, working the dough, and arranging artistic toppings, all used their perspectives together while building mutuality.

Teaching awareness of the Four Approaches became a custom. It gave newcomers a simple system from which to build common ground where they could incorporate their special talents and traits.

The Four Approaches:

NORTH | You enjoy doing things well in a variety of dissimilar situations. Self-critical, you assess the criticism from others to explore your development more deeply. You quickly assess the credentials of your judges, not for their level of authority, but for their merits. It is from here that you decide how to further interact.

Anything you decide to experience becomes a way to improve yourself. You consistently monitor your progress in a subjective way and keep track of your evolution in written or recorded form. Constantly alert to places of weakness, you strive until your weaknesses become strengths. Your conversation style is terse and logical. You dislike conversing about trite subjects. When answering questions you are well organized and fact-oriented.

As with work, you also schedule time for play that benefits your mind and body. You like to follow specific steps and place these in chronological or alphabetical order for later reference. You feel comfortable attending to details with a uniformity of presentation. You enjoy doing things within clear deadlines. Your sensory focus revolves around smell and taste.

For Reference: • Organized • Detail-oriented • Accurate • Perfection-driven • Disciplined • Punctual • Predictable • Follow rules • Sequential procedures • Critical • Rigidly adhere to routines • Emotionally closed • Reason-oriented • Quality-driven

EAST | While exploring, you move in many directions at once. Planning future events satisfies your ability to conceptualize your multi-lateral ideas. Everything is a springboard for designs from which to create innovative productions. You use lively implementation methods to satisfy your creative abilities. You gather abstract ideas and arrange them into clear and distinctive solutions that accomplish the goal fully. Your ideas help others expand their abilities. You have a keen idea of what steps need to be taken.

You are intuitive. You are flexible and tolerant to the idiosyncrasies of others. You must always feel that you have the freedom to do as you wish. Often you enter and spontaneously create emancipated situations and enlivened experiences. After you follow your urges until they subside, you move on to explore other possibilities. You use mechanical tools well and care about how you use your resources. Your quality of life must contain variety, intensity and vitality. Your sensory focus revolves around sight.

For Reference: • Artistically creative • Intuitive • Envisions the total picture quickly • Processes large amounts of data rapidly • Problem-solver • Energetic • Visionary • Multi-talented • Impulsive • Dislikes conflict • Passionate • Enthusiastic • Dislikes slow-paced work • Adaptable • Adventurous • Motivational

SOUTH | Emotional and empathetic; you join, listen attentively, and share feelings in order to express your views about human values and their relationship to personal advancement. You choose to be surrounded by people rather than possessions. You enjoy both the written and spoken word. With strong empathetic powers, you often use your caring ability to seek and cultivate intimacy with individuals and special interest groups. As an observer, you are most happy when an event has meaning beyond its mere experience.

Your environment offers comfort to others, and you desire to make those around you feel appreciated. Relationship-oriented, you may not want to inconvenience your friends with your personal troubles. You enjoy unity, togetherness, and reliability and relish recounting stories that bring your emotions and the emotions of others into harmony. Your sensory associations are through touch and movement. People appreciate your ability to nurture and create concord.

For Reference: • Caring • Compassionate • Enjoys comfort • Enjoys music • Empowers others to achieve their potential • Inspires loyalty • Cooperative • Sentimental • Empathetic • Non-linear•Expressive•Devoted•Warm-hearted•Instructive • Trusting

WEST | You enjoy responsibility and feeling useful as a means to belong to social groups of interest to you. You enjoy traditions and being involved with groups. You are conservative in your actions and attitudes. Technically adept, you quietly come up with realistic solutions. Discriminating and insightful, you organize others and have a talent for clarifying and utilizing gathered information.

Your steadfast attitude is appreciated. You determine your action through a direct approach of evaluating and prioritizing in order to achieve success. Dependable and reliable, your hard work is appreciated. Not interested in delegating work, you diligently complete each task using the knowledge derived from all accumulated information. You consistently set and achieve goals to the best of your skill. You follow the process to the goal and these steps keep you focused. You are quietly competitive and can influence situations to reach your desired outcome. Your sensory focus is hearing.

For Reference: • Logical • Decisive • Confident • Strong-willed • Punctual • Prefers working alone • Impatient • Judgmental • Prefers to hide behind polite remarks rather than show authentic feelings • Practical • Efficient • Disciplined

Sue emphases that sometimes it is difficult to assign a direction to yourself because as one evolves, your style of approach will widen and take on characteristics of opposite cardinal points as well as positive traits from the other groups. When you use a variety of approaches, it signals that you are clarifying your inner strength of mind. Sue suggests that it is advantageous to widen your awareness by learning to identify how people you know approach new situations. Find new ways to interact with those who approach you from different directions. Find examples of people you know who approach from the opposite compass points from you. Do you feel comfortable interacting with all of the four approachers?

CHAPTER FIVE

PLEASURES ENHANCE PERCEPTIONS

One of this summer's interns has agreed to share her experiences as recorded in her black canvas journal.

Inée: When I first turned to drive up My Way of Growing Wheel International for the Volunteer Gardening Week event, I had no idea that I was going to meet with someone as extraordinary as Sue Gurnee. I had been invited through a mutual friend to help out, and I was never told exactly who this woman with a garden was.

I arrived at the property unsure of where I was, or what I was going to be doing. I parked in the indicated grass lot and got out of the car and sighed. It was a lovely, green, welcoming environment and something in me stirred with wonder. I simply felt so at home. There was no one to greet me, and as far as I saw, there wasn't anybody around at all. I didn't know where to go so I figured I could just wait. I climbed to the top of my car and lay open, looking at the clouds and the sun.

Soon after, I met Sue and I gathered that she was a very powerful individual indeed. She is a healer of a very special sort. She was born with heightened sense perception and can see the energies and auras that encircle everything. I had so many questions, but since I had never met an Energy Healer before, I did not want to ask a silly or untactful question so I did my best to listen and glean. I asked her if she needed a volunteer for July and a part of August.

I really felt that I was led to meet her through a divine force, and by following this guidance, I will open my horizons to incredible opportunities never imagined by my limited scope of mind. She said that she did, in fact, need a volunteer and we agreed that I would come to help her with anything she needed for the time I was here.

Nothing could have prepared me for the immense cloud of knowledge and learning that would immerse me in a field of understanding that I never knew existed. Knowing this now, I am sure that I would more eagerly jump into these mysterious waters, but as a naïve intern, I approached this incredible journey with caution, but an infinitely open mind.

-Inée

When interns settle into living in cabins dotted around the hundred mountainous acres of forest and flower-filled pastures, they begin to organize mental awareness files. These files are the basis of awareness expansion. Beyond the mental labels such as the person from Persia, the gal with a back tattoo, or that guy with a new car, Sue teaches interns about structuring sensory information. This includes, voice, smell, touch, and even the size and shape of their footprints. This form of awareness filing is made possible by practicing methods to consciously organize the incoming sensory information into that which is Specific and building awareness to elements that are Ambient.

"Specific shows you what—and the ambient tells you where. For example, using your senses of sight, hearing, touch, smell and taste, and focus on, the taste of an apple picked from this tree on the hill, the specific is the flavor and the ambient would be the other senses—the ones that are the lesser focused upon while chewing the first bite. Examples of things you could bring into focus might be the feeling of your toe in your shoe while standing on the hill; the sound of the young people next door playing outside, or the smell of the straw wafting this way from the chicken coop. These are all ambient until you direct your attention there. With practice you can expand your specifics and ambient awareness to include multitudes of simultaneously comprehensible information. While you taste the apple, you can also hear the bees and know their processes; feel the weather and life force of the apple while identifying the fruity fragrance of the apple leaves…while looking the laden branches. The specific and the ambient information as it is attained through the five senses filters through a part of your brain called the Reticular Activating System. This filtered information is then is sent through your Limbic System, the seat of emotions, and is processed in your unique way in both hemispheres of your brain.

"With just minutes of directed sensory training each day, you can build sensory files that contain extremely detailed specific and ambient information. Orderly files sharpen your connection to each moment. Orderly files strengthen your short and long-term memory. Orderly files help you discern a wide range of subtleties from which you can enhance your intuition!"

Interns quickly get used to Sue's information-filled lectures while they are engaged in such commonplace activities as repairing fencing or weeding garden paths.

Inée: Sue's lessons can be given at any time, any place. Sometimes a simple question about how the human mind operates, or how energy works, turns into a full lecture. This might be while organizing the cutlery and dishes for a luncheon for thirty guests, or while weeding together in the garden.

"It is with your five senses that you experience your world. The more you train your senses, the more accurately you take in specific and ambient information. You are a product of this cataloged information. When your awareness files match the actuality of a situation, your accurate retrieval can be called, for our purposes – 100. As you continue to widen your awarenesses, this measured 100 continues to intensify. When your sensory input filing and retrieval register under 100, it signals that your subjective reactions and responses are actually giving misinformation to your conscious mind. Accurate awareness filing is what Sue teaches daily.

Inée asks: What is the connection between sensory stimuli and my intuition?

"Your sensory training prepares you to effortlessly gather

meta-sensory details. Like remembering the color or texture of an object, you will soon be able to retrieve intuitional details from flashes of insight with similar vividness. Orderly filing specific and ambient information of the five senses and also from subtle energies are foundational for training your intuition. When you are relaxed and have access to all levels of incoming information, then you can fortify your inner wisdom."

Inée: Well, how do you fortify your inner wisdom?

"I believe that a most supportive way is to build into each moment: authentic enjoyment.

Enjoyment may seem superfluous and superficial. To be enjoyable, an experience must be complex enough to the degree that you engage yourself and discover new potentials. The process of enjoyment often is the process of withdrawing attention from generalized external stimuli and directing the attention to the input as it comes into the physical senses. When you allow only what you wish to admit into your awareness, you derive a form of pleasure. This teaches you about the specific. The ambient is the housing for your sustained pleasures. This helps you to include more and more into your specific file so you can keep track of it without wavering.

"Everything the body can do is potentially enjoyable. Often we forget the amount of pleasure that is available in every moment. If your physical senses are underdeveloped, you receive confused information without the adequate amount of content to be considered pleasurable. This likewise, can stunt the growth of your inner wisdom.

"An untrained, unsteady body cannot build enjoyable interpretation into its movements. An insensitive eye misses interpretations of specific and ambient information and thus presents uninteresting evidence to the mind's recollections. An unmusical ear receives jarring noises and cannot build order or interpretation. The coarse palate experiences insipid tastes; hence, one finds little enjoyment from dining at gourmet restaurants. As you bring order and sensitivity to physical sensations, your enjoyment increases and so can your intuition.

"Make a joyful noise! Use your senses in a way that connects you to the miracles that you are: the miracles of your being."

Inée: Sue handed me a packet of information to read about the history of the property as well as guidelines for my stay. Before she left she mentioned:

"The word 'dilettante' comes from the Latin word delectare – to find delight in. May the work you do during your internship serve to delight and fulfill your senses at every moment."

Inée: This morning Sue took me to the 4th of July Liberty Parade in Todd after she showed me what my duties are going to be. She gave me a special "stripe bag" with notecards, a pen, and a lighter. The notecards indicated what tasks I need to work on. There were ongoing activities like garden tending, trail maintenance, post office duties, and chicken care; and there were smaller projects such as cleaning and organizing an area, or moving things around the property. After the intern intro, we headed to Todd to see the festivities.

Well, I ended up being involved in the parade. How it works is that local artists make costumes and beautiful banners, flags, puppets, and lanterns and the community can just join in the annual parade. I saw many of my beloved Boone friends and Baha'i friends. The parade has a theme: the Elements, Earth, Air, Fire, and Water. This year the focus was Air. All elements were in the parade, but Air was leading the march. I dressed up in a blue cape and carried a lovely towering white lantern of paper. I was with the Air clan. There were many others dressed in outfits of water, earth, and fire. There were fish and birds and bears and all sorts of animal puppets and paper decorations. We marched down the main street, stopped in a moment of silence to listen to the creek running parallel to our march, and then continued into the heart of Todd. We stopped again where the spectators were and sang the Star Spangled Banner together, then continued to the park where a skit was planned. We circled round and round the park until all participants were together. It was a cheerful event.

Back at Growing Wheel, I was given the assignment to clean and organize the fridge in the House of Five Senses (HoFS) and to feed the chickens some old peaches and apples. I devised a tile platform for the chickens to eat off of and not to scratch so much hay into their food. Sue liked it a lot. After cleaning the fridge, our neighbor and her boyfriend came over to invite me to go kayaking down the river. I was reluctant because I thought I needed to work but Sue gave me permission and said, "…there is always time for fun." We floated down 6 miles of river quietly and I enjoyed the lovely sun and air and the nature all around me. Very beautiful day.

-Inée

Chapter Six

PLEASURE AND FULFILLMENT

Inée: Watching me while I swept the walkway to the garden, Sue began a morning lesson about the energetic components of pleasure, enjoyment, and fulfillment.

"If you hold an inability to fully accept sustained enjoyment, perhaps it is due to a pseudo-conclusion that you must override pleasures with guilt feelings about having feelings. I am convinced that pleasure and enjoyment are authentic needs. These authentic needs of an adult may be repressed due to a belief that sustained pleasures are wrong and must not to be pursued. Desires that are authentic may be detoured. You may actually have trained your body not to feel pleasure unless as a reward for being good or doing something of merit.

"Sensory pleasures available through sight, smell, taste, hearing, and touch, may actually be dulled due to false conclusions.

"Since the circles of desire and fulfillment have expanded in the past hundred years, perhaps we will gain new categories for simple pleasures that are holistic and pure. There is a correlation between allowing pleasure and the topic of destructiveness.

"When people think of pleasure, there may be a link to pain and inner destructiveness. Then they obviously think of something that is bad–destruction being bad, creation being good. So when we observe thinking, feeling actions, we look for destructiveness. It's very common to want to look at where, in a dualistic view, you did something wrong. For example, where you broke something or weren't 'good'. But in actuality, your destructive and creative aspects are of the same power. The power of energetics.

"Your own five senses hold a myriad of pleasure in a natural flow. The pleasure of living in your magnificent body while using it in healthy ways – that is such a pleasure. How you evaluate that pleasure, interestingly enough, when not in its natural flow, usually holds a degree of self-destructiveness. This can be found, as it is something that is impeding the natural flow of energy.

"In any way when the flow is interfered with, this energy expression is blocked. How you shift around your own inner sensibility so that you can take any experience and move it into the place of pleasure is what your creative ability can do. For example, if the conditions on the outside are such that there is sun on your back or wind blowing dust into your eyes, it wakes up your inner constructiveness or inner destructiveness to decide what to do. Adjust or in a small way, suffer.

"You can either choose to work with or avoid and separate/ ignore input in some way. But what happens is often when you make the choice, either to be in the receptive principle and accept it and shift things around for it, or the action principle where we decide to make a change; the element that is destructive in that is the element of the critical energy. The criticalness.

"So, when something happens instead of moving into the understanding that it is one power, there is actually an inner block that is built, from separating yourself inside, to become critical of the other part of you and what it is doing. This inner constructiveness is apparent when all of a sudden the constructiveness velcro-ed together with the criticalness, while wanting to make some kind of evaluation, absolutely turns into hostility.

"Nervous stress and the mask of hostility are signals that somehow you are blocking the pleasure that is available in the moment if you tune into the specifics of your senses. Check if you are afraid of your pleasure because your own pleasure is in a negative state. Meaning that you want to have the pleasure, the secondary gain of something that feels good to you, but you also have the critical creative attitude that if you are unhappy, it shows how wrong another is as you are not getting what you want.

"So you blame someone else and then get some pleasure. You gain a subtle form of pleasure from that and so you don't have to look for the creative or the larger unified flow of pleasure. Well what happens on some level of consciousness, it builds guilt. And this is the guilt against the idea of having pleasure, just pure pleasure, like sitting in a chair, listening to little crickets, playing with a cat, feeling the softness of the cat's fur as you stroke it softly, et cetera.

"So you repress pleasure and as you repress it you repress all types of feelings and can go numb! Numb to feelings, numb to pleasure, while remaining seemingly fine on the mental level. You avoid pleasure that is not a mental activity. Sensory pleasure, in some level of your consciousness, is filed as a gateway to self-destructiveness. This is against nature's design.

"If pleasure and real or imagined self-destructiveness are intertwined, it's going to be difficult to want to access pleasure. Here is why. In all of nature, pleasure and life force are intertwined. Natural things that make you want to continue life and life's expressions seal pleasure and life together. But if self-destructiveness and pleasure of life force are together, something has to be numb to keep the support. Because of that, most of the time people will want to avoid pleasure so that they avoid self-destructiveness. This affects the life force.

"This is very much involved with what psychology focuses on through stories and models. Often the energetic component is overlooked. Self-destructiveness is not bad. Positive attitude is not good. From the energetic viewpoint it is all one flow. Using the five senses and using the pleasure that's available through the five senses, tensions can relax and stresses lessen. If you need to access pleasure and feel compromised in doing so you may hold a five senses frustration. Yet, you still need to feel pleasure and you feel this pleasure through destructiveness.

"This destructiveness can either be self-directed or imposed on others. And this is very interesting because you can comprehend the painful outer situations that may not actually relate to your needs or your numbness. It gives (not directly) the subconscious and the unconscious a feeling of rebellion towards the actuality of the situation. Through dowsing, you can find where the destructive connections are. Most often these are not directly sexual, but often sensuous, which jump into a sexual context–as wants. The available five senses, and their innumerable gratifications, are somewhat numbed and often not reawakened.

"You don't even have to look far to find something that causes pleasure to your senses. Try this now. What do you feel, see, and hear? Pleasures are within your reach. But any pleasures can be overlaid with the need to feel special. This hidden need is actually very interesting. It is, I believe, a hidden need to triumph over others. To triumph over others means to be against others because you have a false notion that 'I am over them, I am separate from them as I feel superior. They are there. I am here. I will have more pleasure. This makes me (dualistically) good and better than others.'

"So when you feel that you have gained some degree of mastery, there is often a separation that follows this growth. 'Ah, look at how far I've gotten.' This destructiveness is again a very subtle self-analysis or criticism. It destroys the building of noble values because it is a subjective or separated attitude. It is impossible for you to measure your uniqueness against others.

"Because you're bringing out a part of yourself that is pushing or pulling to be something other than what you are, there is a focus not to maintain pleasure but to bring some form of pain. This, in your mind makes you feel superior and pleasure-filled. Yes. The self-destructive separation causes you a form of pleasure while losing connection to the unified life force.

"So the questions you can ask are, 'Where am I not honest with life? Where am I not honest with my own sensory pleasures? Where do I cheat, and when I cheat, where do I lessen my integrity?' Wherever pure pleasure is rejected, integrity is impaired.

"My working definition of the lack of integrity is: the personal impediment of sensory or cognitive flow due to the separation of parts within the self. This destroys the unity of your energetic being. When you trust yourself in whatever you're doing, as you're doing it, this allows continued expansion. Integrity is the trust that this expansion widens your ability to be spontaneous as well as your capacity to accept the pleasures of each moment.

"Check if you believe that if someone else has pleasure that there is less for you. And in the abundant world, ask yourself 'where am I the co-producer of this situation? Where have I negated something? Have I used a short-cut that is actually part of the pleasure flow, that has been either negated inside myself, or caused destructiveness to myself or others?'

"When you search for the answers, release any beliefs that you are bad. If at any time, you use a limited, moralistic, or even a trained platitude, and you conclude that you are bad, consider the following...

Ask yourself:

• What are your reasons for acting submissive or aggressive?
• Are you feeling self-assured enough to ask questions?
  If not, why?
• Do you feel that you deserve to have fulfillment?

I have categorized nine authentic needs of an adult that keep your focus on constructive patterns. You can use this chart as a guide from which to make decisions that facilitate sustained pleasures that are healthy and pure."

Sue provided Inée with some study materials for her journal.

The Authentic Needs of an Adult

• Pleasure
• Growth and Development
• Love
• Self-expression
• Companionship
• Intimate relationships
• Making meaningful contributions
• Fulfillment
• Reaching one's spiritual potentials and
  everything that accrues from that

Inée was intrigued. After some thought, she could not hold back this question: When I was in high school we were introduced to Maslow's Hierarchy of Needs. What do you think of this model?

"Interesting you mentioned his pioneer study. Abraham Maslow was a psychologist who proposed in the 1940's, a hypothesis about motivation. He did this after studying college students. He used the themes similar to the ones on your most recent handout. My energetic observations have brought me to different conclusions of the hierarchy of desires of college-aged interns and the dynamics of their growth and development.

"Maslow's linear approach to self-realization and fulfillment did not include the language of energetics and the host of multi-dimensional fulfillments that the power of energetics can bring.

"With many psychology-oriented students learning Maslow's developmental road map, a mass consciousness vibration has formed that may actually – in a most subtle manner – detour the path of one's personal multi-dimensional fulfillment.

"The list I gave you is significant. All the lessons I teach here help you bring the energetic components of fulfillment into your life. You can clearly recognize your authentic needs.

"When I help you to focus your attention toward the disturbances that may be in your energy system it is to hasten the development of your authentic fulfillment.

"My view is holistic. After satisfying the basics of attaining food, water, sleep, and the needs of the body, the evolution of an energy-savvy person exponentially expands. Themes such as: personal security, communications with family members, the definitions of prosperity, and the freedom to continue friendships across the globe, will grant more opportunities for energy-focused fulfillments than ever before. These open you to wider arenas from which to share your love and a sense of belonging with wider levels of self-realization.

"Maslow postulated self-esteem, confidence, achievement, respect of others, and a sense of place. These were ripened by only a few who could reach the top of his theory's pyramid.

"Twenty-five years after his theory was accepted, many self-help books, confidence-building seminars, and leadership conferences packed seminar halls on a weekly basis. College-aged students were weaned on the importance of realizing creativity, spontaneity, problem-solving, and acceptance. Therapists wore out leather couches helping young adults to find fulfillment to subjective deficiencies."

I wonder what Maslow would have written about if he lived 75 years longer. The apex of his pyramid of development ended with the attainment of a peak experience and transcendence. Now this can be a lifestyle.

The complex brains of interns who come here begin the foundation of their hierarchy with parallel developmental motivations. Personal and financial security, health, and well-being are easier to maintain once the energetic components are understood. Interns learn methods to incorporate the laws of nature into the attainment of their desires. The acquisition of safety and security are quickly understood the first day the interns arrive.

They learn the comfort of cabins without electricity and they gain a direct connection to the water sources by knowing where the aquifers are. They build respect for the amount of time it takes to grow a straight carrot, or to nurture chickens before an egg can come to the table. These simple experiences set the pace for fulfillment in a most memorable manner.

Social needs depend on circumstances. These may differ from culture to culture due to the collective histories or collective beliefs in any group.

Inée: Is it possible for a person's ideals to affect the masses and actually dissipate my own energetic power?

"Energies born from education, that affect collective consciousness may be a form of collective mediocrity. They may not reflect your pure desires. You become entranced by what I define as conceptualized gratifications (those that are not personal but adopted unknowingly from others in your group). You lose your individuality and are not aware that you are following a pattern of someone who is living or not living.

"I think most high school students in the US have been taught Maslow's view. Therefore, these manifested needs and conceptualized gratifications result from mass and collective consciousness or from energetic overlays.

"From my sight, imposed desires hold vibrational signatures that are not congruent with your individual energy frequency. Any non-congruent energy conglomerate scatters your personal creative power. It affects you. This is an externally-driven pseudo-reality version of what you need for your authentic fulfillment."

Inée: By using the list of authentic needs that Sue gave me, I have begun to see things differently. It is imperative that now I explore the reasons why I may prevent myself from feeling pleasure, which is one of the nine authentic needs. My exploration will bring me more understanding, and this understanding may help me to release those inner tensions that may have previously held me back. So far as I have interned here, I have learned to stop and observe the environment around me on a more regular basis.

Before, I would be so rushed and busy that I would rarely take the time to really slow down, to identify the individual smells in the air, or to put evocative words on what I was feeling physically or emotionally. Simply by making deeper observations, I have improved my sensory awareness. I'll take my own novice advice: If something feels good, smells good, looks good, tastes good, sounds good – I will take a moment to attach distinct and specific reasons to WHY it pleases me. All the more, if there is a situation where I feel uncomfortable, unsure, frightened, or reluctant – that is all okay. I need to find out more about those feelings and not hesitate to explore and engage the immense spectrum of physical and emotional sensations I am capable of.

I received such metaphorical pleasures from one of my recent observations:

It was an overcast day. The bugs sent a constant symphony of trills to weave through the cool wild breeze. I was walking barefoot from my little Garden Hut and stopped on my way to HoFS by a very curious sight. A large twitchy wasp was dragging an equally large brown spider across the gravel driveway. I didn't want to get too close to disturb this strange natural occurrence but I was still able to notice details.

The wasp was no ordinary brown house wasp. He had a big body about an inch long, and spindly, slender legs. His metal-like exoskeleton gleamed cobalt blue in the light and his clear wings were tipped with yellow and were constantly trembling in his movements. I first thought the pair was fighting, but the wasp released the spider briefly, and she stood still.

She was about the same size as the wasp, brown with a soft body, and long slim legs covered in tiny villous hairs. She had her first two legs open wide and above her head, as if to embrace her enemy. I was surprised she didn't move and assumed that she must have been paralyzed just prior to my discovery of them. She seemed like she was under a spell. I could not decide which creature I would have preferred to live, but I was sympathetic for the spider. I found it easy to side with the victim and maybe that mirrors how I feel in general.

I found it rather odd that the wasp chose to drag her by her mouth. It was an awkward dance of predator and prey and I watched them for a few minutes. The grass was sharp on the soles of my feet, and the rocks pressed into my heels uncomfortably. I felt a pang of pity for the spider as I watched her soft belly drag across rocks and cut grass. She didn't stand much of a chance against the metal-bodied wasp. He was taking her with some determination across the gravel and towards the garden. Maybe he was going to feed a wasp-baby, I thought. Maybe his actions were justified but I don't know the full story. I wanted to follow them but knowing that it wasn't a happy ending, I uprooted my eyes and continued with my day.

As I look back on this commentary, I find it rather interesting that I assigned the female gender to the spider, and the male gender to the wasp. I am no entomologist so I wouldn't usually be able to determine the sex of an insect; I assigned those genders so that it would be easier to refer to the creatures as "he" or "she" in the writing.

If I look deeper, perhaps I could've been projecting my feelings of victimization by a man onto the she-spider because inwardly I may feel like I was the victim in a past situation. Could I be attributing the qualities of aggression and violence to men because I wrote that the wasp was male? Exercising my ability to take pleasure in observing my surroundings is helping me better understand myself.

-Inée

"One frequent sensory pleasure is derived from touch. If the energetic component of this sense is not supportive, touching may not hold full pleasure to the one who is being touched."

Inée: In the Energy Awareness class, Sue explained that sometimes when people touch you, they leave their energy. Their essence, or a notion, from their body can circulate into your energy system during the impulse of touching. Even professional people: massage therapists, dentists, and manicurists can leave their essence. Since everyone has their own unique energy signature, this can be inhibiting to people and their energy fields.

Sue presented an exercise to teach us how to touch without leaving a "fingerprint" on others. I was partnered with Ian and everyone else was paired. Sue instructed person A to place one hand on our partner's leg on the quadriceps muscle, then to remove the hand. She asked if person B still felt the hand on their leg. Ian said yes. I was a little embarrassed. Then she instructed person A to touch again and take our energy back. I concentrated with eyes closed and visualized my energy returning to my hand. Then removed my hand. Ian said he still felt my energy, so I tried again. I was a little nervous now.

After I tried a second time to remove my energy, Ian said that it felt "clean". That he still felt something, but it was different. The point is not to feel the weight left from where the hand touched. This is an exercise about energy. Ian didn't feel the energy anymore and Sue said that she saw that I did it! So interesting. Now Ian's turn—he has worked with energy before so he really has a lot of experience. He put a hand on my leg and when he removed his hand, I still felt it – maybe it was the residual heat. He had a warm hand. He returned his hand to take the energy back and when he removed it, it definitely felt different. It was a tiny bit tingly, but mostly cool.

Now we upgraded the exercise and sent energy down into the leg from our hand. The energy went through the skin, muscle, bone, and reached the bone marrow level. We were to send energy down to that level and bring it back out again. I didn't know what I was doing really but I closed my eyes and concentrated. I visualized my energy going down to the bone marrow, and then lifted it out. When I removed my hand, Ian said he felt the energy in the muscle level; I hadn't pulled it all out yet. I put my hand back and concentrated.

The second time Ian said it felt clear and Sue confirmed. I never knew I was capable of such things. Now it's Ian's turn. I tried to be aware of what level the energy was at, but again, since I am new to this, I don't know if I was perceptive enough to keep up with it clearly.

When he removed his hand, I told Sue I had trouble separating the energy sensation from the sensation of heat from his hand. Ian did it again, just hovering his hand over my leg and it felt cool, like my skin was experiencing a cold breeze. Sue said that this coolness is the body's autonomic response to the energy because it has never experienced energy going to that level in such a way.

Upgrade the exercise again: face each other and send energy through both hands into both legs, and pull it back again. When I did this, Ian said he still felt energy in his right leg. Sue said it was because I haven't practiced moving energy with my left hand yet (I had been using my right hand this whole time). I replaced my left hand and called my energy back. Ian said it felt better. Then we briefly sent energy into each other's arms.

Sue noticed that when I'm receiving energy, she sees my energy draw back a little, as if afraid. She told me not to be afraid. I wonder why this is. Could it be that I'm afraid to get close to people? Was it just Ian's energy specifically, or energy in general that I was reacting to?

-Inée

CHAPTER SEVEN

MUSCLE-RESPONSE TESTING

Inée: Since we use dowsing as part of our ongoing research, I was elated when Sue asked me:

"Would you like to use muscle-response testing to find answers about your authentic needs beyond your conscious awareness?"

She told me that muscle-response testing can be used:

• As a communication method from inner realms of your unique being to your conscious mind and

• As a verification signal those inner energetic changes have occurred.

Muscle-response testing establishes a very convenient system to gain information from your many levels of consciousness. When used properly, muscle-response testing can be an accurate detector of hidden truths. The parts of the mind that control the autonomic functions of the body can be programmed to keenly locate inconsistencies in your attitudes, concepts, and beliefs. Skill in the use of muscle-response testing comes from practice, the consistent ability to remain neutral, and the respectful use of this personal tool.

Inée: I woke up at 8:00 and said the Long Obligatory Prayer on the front deck of my little hut; it was beautiful. I am aching for my hiking boots and I feel forlorn without them. At about 11:45 this morning, I went to town, got my boots at my storage unit, grabbed some zip-ties for rope lights, and picked up mail. I also went to thrift stores to find some work clothes. I very timidly asked, "Hey Sue, I don't want to be untactful but...what exactly are you capable of?" She smiled and told me.

She had a gift for healing since she was young and her grandfather was a healer. She said she has had multitudes of students and that there is no set curriculum or lesson plan because everyone progresses at different rates. It has to do with aptitude and interest. I told her I would be very interested in learning. With energy healing, she is able to "see" into an injury (as one would with an x-ray), and she can detect pre-dispositions to diseases up to six or seven generations back.

She uses muscle-response testing (dowsing) daily. I asked her where the answers come from. She said that the answers come from a central source of Truth, like a universal pool of answers. I wondered if it has anything to do with personal intuition, and Sue replied that they are unrelated, that it is knowledge that is accessible by all.

She gifted me her book ***Chain of Diamonds*** earlier today and it looks very interesting. From what I can glean from glancing through it, it is about balancing oneself by carefully placing certain plants in a 12'x12' garden to amplify different energies within. I feel like I'm getting the hang of the routine pretty quickly, but it still is a bit overwhelming. I enjoy the work here and I hope I will contribute to her ongoing projects and be of service in the utmost. I feel so very good about being here.

-Inée

Today's lesson enhanced my understanding about desires and fulfillments...

"If you consider that in every reaction and response lies a desire, it would follow logically that when you become crystal clear about your own reactions, you gain deeper understanding of your unique and innermost desires."

In a few minutes, Sue took off her jacket and began a new lesson.

"Get your water bottle. Drink some water. A few gulps are enough. I am going to give you the most glorious tool that you will be able to carry with you wherever you go. Step right up, stand please."

Full Body Technique | For a **yes** answer, you will program your body when standing, to lean forward slightly as if a gentle breeze is blowing across your shoulders from behind. For a **no** answer, your body will sway backward slightly. Practice these forward and backward motions a few times while simultaneously installing the thought that **yes** is the forward movement and **no** is a backward movement as you make these movements. When you feel the pattern is set after a few times of swaying forward and backward, ask your body to show you the yes and no responses. When your body automatically answers **yes** with the forward motion and **no** with a backward motion, your programming is complete and this step will not have to be done again.

When you wish to use this method of dowsing, stand with your feet hip width apart and your knees slightly bent. Envision yourself connected to the earth with strength streaming down through your legs and exiting from the balls of your feet through the location called Bubbling Springs – acupuncture point K1. Then imagine a connection of a brilliant shaft of energy streaming into your crown chakra at the top of your head and the flow of electromagnetic energy lightly enveloping you. Ask to be given a **yes** and a **no** response to check that you are in correct polarity. Let your body give you the **yes** response with a tilt forward and the **no** response with a backward sway. Ask if your dowsing is accurate and reliable.

Inée: Before dowsing, Sue informed me that there are a couple things to set up. First you must establish a set of basic "pre-programs" as a form of mutual understanding between you and your dowsing system. For instance, if you are going to dowse, "Is there any foreign energy left on me that is interfering with my energy field?" your definitions of "foreign" and "interfering" may differ from what the dowsing system understands them as. You need to set up these "pre-programs" only once, and then you and the dowsing system will be on the same page.

The next requirement before you start is to ask three initial questions. These are simple questions that will help you test for hidden problems in your dowsing system, and prevent you from getting random answers. Below is a further explanation of the questions. It is very important to remain detached from these answers, meaning not to hope for a YES or a NO. If one has expectations or ideas of how one wants it to be, then the purpose of dowsing for guidance is moot.

Sue showed me a list of pre-programs to help set up my dowsing system. Think of these programs as rules to play a game. If all players (you and your dowsing system) understand the same set of rules, the game can be played fairly and without conflict. If, however, the players were taught different ways to play, there will be much misunderstanding during the game-play.

Here is what Sue showed me:

Setting your Pre-Programs | Included are four basic pre-programs to energetically install into your personal dowsing program. This is achieved by simply reading each one aloud. Don't worry if the programs don't make sense at this time. These will stay in your system until you desire to make changes. These will become part of all future dowsing activity. These four samples act as your foundation:

• Dowsing Accuracy Program
• Universal Truth Program
• Privacy Program
• Dowsing System Term Use Program

1. Dowsing Accuracy Program | "This program is continually to be in effect until I consciously choose to make changes. This program includes the primary controls, limits, agreements, and dowsing responses I engage in. This program is designed to override my free will responses. This program will adjust my whole being's ability to maintain the highest accuracy when receiving answers to my requested information. This information is to be accessed from the place of all Truth and given to me in a way that I can understand through the Dowsing System. Time, as related to dowsing answers, is to be given to me in the time zone where I stand while dowsing."

2. Universal Truth Program | "This program is continually to be in effect until I consciously choose to make changes. This program strengthens my alignment with the laws of physics and the laws of nature that apply while using dowsing as a means to correct discord within my system. This overrides cultural, habitual, familial and all other subjective pseudo-solutions to the highest and most appropriate outcome for growth and development according to my divine plan."

3. Privacy Program | "This program is continually to be in effect until I consciously choose to make changes. This program includes the ethical support to protect myself and others while dowsing. Privacy, within myself and others, allows that information not appropriate to obtain using dowsing will result in the inability to receive either a yes or no answer signaling that the question is not an appropriate dowsing question."

4. Dowsing System Term Use Program | "This program is continually to be in effect until I consciously choose to make changes. This program includes the working definitions of these (and other terms that I subsequently define) while involved in dowsing. Examples for this pre-program include but are not limited to: **Cleared** is to mean that the many sources and types of discordant energies or influences have been neutralized to a degree that is registered as inner balance. I am ready to move to another topic. **Balanced** is to mean that all of the multi-dimensional aspects included in this topic have found a supportive manner to help me achieve my highest potential for my growth and development. **Are there**... is meant that in the past 28 days I have the environmental conditions accumulated to a degree that.... **Structure** as used in dowsing terms is meant to include an energetic, mental, physical, or emotional block or crosscurrents of energies keeping me from attaining my goal. **Light** is to mean ketheric or divine power that purifies and reorganizes those elements that are discordant. When appropriate, new definitions will be added as needed to this program. Once acknowledged these will become part of the pre-program until I update a definition for further clarity." *Please remember: if your question contains a word or group of words that have assumed or conflicting meanings that you and your Dowsing System have not agreed upon, then your dowsing answer may be random.*

Pre-Program 3

Step 2 Asking three questions | Before engaging in a dowsing session, there is a protocol that must be observed. If not, you could get a random answer. Since dowsing uses a binary system it cannot explain further than its binary language. By asking three questions before you begin a session, you test for hidden problems within your dowsing system. These questions were conceived by a group of master dowser members of an organization called the American Society of Dowsers that has advocated for accuracy development since 1961 when it was formed. When you ask simply: **Should I?** implies, considering all aspects related to this situation, is there an answer that can be found? **May I?** means do I have appropriate permission to ask about this topic? **Can I?** asks if I have the inner balance to achieve accurate answers. If you receive a NO to any (or all) of these three questions, stop. Ask inquiring questions to find the specific reason. Detachment is a key to accuracy during the dowsing process. If you feel emotionally involved in an answer you can become a surrogate and influence the outcome of the test even if you have programmed yourself to remove personal feelings and free will. Bring yourself 100% to the present. Then move into a place of detached neutrality. From there your accuracy will become reliable. Ask again, "Should I?, May I?, Can I?" Did that help you to receive a YES answer?

About Asking Questions A common joke among dowsers is that it takes twenty minutes to learn to dowse and twenty years to learn to ask the right questions.

"Even seasoned dowsers can make mistakes by not stating questions in succinct ways. I still have to smile when I tell how I personally know about this. I was asked by a group of health practitioners near Flagstaff, Arizona, if I would locate where to place their new healing center's well. Generously, I offered to teach a mini-course on dowsing. Eager students dressed in hiking boots, windbreakers and backpacks met me on top of a windy bluff. They showed me a map and I clearly explained the steps of finding water with the map and pointed where I felt drilling would be the best. The group gathered near me saying they wanted to use L-rods and walk the land. The target was simple. We were looking for the location for a well. I have a standard pre-program that includes that the 'water is to be less than 300 feet deep, can supply to the surface, a minimum of 3 gallons per minute and it satisfies all legal and drilling requirements. This water must have a reliable source that will provide potable water now and into the future.' Because I spent time teaching each step, there were many thought forms moving around the group. While answering questions and spreading my focus in many directions I casually said 'direct me to the reliable source of water' assuming that I was prepared without asking the proper questions. The geology of the area was not difficult to read. I was receiving erratic dowsing answers. Why? A broad smile cracked across my face. I had not asked the question clearly. In the backpacks of all the students were plastic containers of water bottled 'from a reliable source that will provide potable water now and into the future.' According to my pre-program, their water was less than 300 feet deep. In a minute it could supply the students with the 3 gallons of water, and satisfied the legal and drilling requirements. They just had to dig into their backpacks!"

Chapter Eight

MINDFULNESS AND AMBITIONS

"To fulfill any life ambition – you must remain mindful. The more you are attentive to your desires, the easier it is to then learn to tune into your inner guidance every step of the way. This helps you to take the directed energy and let the creative power pour from you. When you are mindful about how you may hold back your fullness you allow a new form of inner dialog. It can go something like this:

"I can create a new condition here to move past this fear. I feel it is not necessary to be afraid. I have the courage to fully feel my feelings that may include joy, pleasure or perhaps some disappointment or pain, and I know in a wholesome way I can let the energy of positive creation work though me in each step. I can feel any experience and discern the illusion of what I believe the steps are supposed to be like. Then I have the ability to accept them free of subjective overlays. I can indeed share with generosity, abundance, joyousness, and fulfillment while attaining the goals I seek. It begins with the power to support the moment just as it is. Then, I can better strengthen my moment-to-moment decision-making abilities.

"Muscle-response testing is a wonderful tool to help you keep accounting of your authentic desires and what are desires that may have somehow been superimposed due to a subtle fear of accepting the fullness of what can be yours.

"Observe your responses as well as your desires. Make a conscious commitment to your personal progress. Open your inner receptors to file information from the specific and ambient. Let sensory and meta-sensory pleasures help you build sustained and creative fulfillment. Both of these categories of pleasures are found by assessing the scope of your thoughts, your topics of speech, the grace of your actions, the consistency of your effort, the configuration of your ethics, the subtlety of your awareness, and support of your concentration, you can gain mastery."

Use your muscle-testing skills to investigate these topics:

• Resources, Talents, and Proficiencies (the strengths that I have)
• Responses I give (as gifts with my words)
• Critical vs. assessment thoughts (how these energetically affect the connections)
• Topics I choose to talk about with others
• Graceful actions and movements (are all parts of my body free from rigidity?)
• The consistency of my efforts (procrastinations)
• Morals and ethics (holding boundaries)
• Widened awareness (specific and ambient, 5 senses)
• Concentration and focus (holding the levels)
• Healthy pleasures (my authentic needs)
• Energetic training (making energies part of daily life)

Consider keeping a journal of your progress.

Inée: Learning mindfulness began in the garden. "You look like you live here!" Sue said to me this morning. I was out hanging the rope lights around the patio of HoFS, which we named Delphi. I was wearing my overall shorts, a cut off shirt and my big garden sun hat. I guess I have settled in this environment well. I FEEL like I live here and that I've been here for a long time. She gave me a really great morning lecture about being open and accepting.

She said, "The inability to fulfill authentic needs is often based on rigidity." Some people are so set in their ways that they are closed to changing or a different way of thinking. She explained that some people live in duality: either they are the best, or they feel they are nothing – they equate **not** being the best with being dead. If you're not first, then you must be last sort of mentality. When they fail, they see nothing left – dead. So to compensate they may manipulate others into loving them to avoid punishment or punishing themselves. It is a very good point, and a new thing to become compassionate about in those people who use this dualistic criticism of themselves.

I believe that everyone needs to receive love and compassion, but when someone starts to take advantage of that kindness and becomes a poison in your life, you must be careful not to let that poison weaken you. It may be necessary to distance yourself. We deserve to be surrounded by the people we love and who UPLIFT our spirit and bring our hearts joy.

Anyway, the idea of no electricity in my room is more and more appealing to me as the days pass. I can use the computer when I go into Boone for Internet and I can listen to music on my phone if I absolutely have to. Settling down at night with a book or this journal by candlelight is very peaceful. It's a new experience of being unplugged that I fully accept. I don't think I even want to dig that power line from the Sundown Theater anymore.

After the morning lesson, I got a full tour of the lovely Diamond Garden. She explained that there are three parts to the make up of the garden: the body, mind, and spirit. Each relates to the diamond-shaped raised beds. Each had a collection of joyful plants growing. There is also the "Silent Garden", a place in the corner that is "so quiet we forget about it." It has zucchini and melon plants. I was practicing muscle-response testing to find where to start my weeding work. I got a NO to the carrot and tomato beds, the Mind, Spirit and Body Gardens, a NO to the empty weeded patch, and a NO to the garden near the pond. I did get a YES to start clearing weeds in the Silent Garden.

I started weeding between the zucchini, melon, and marigolds. Sue said to move the marigolds, which were being shaded by the zucchini's giant leaves, to a different location. There were five marigolds being shaded and I dowsed to find that three of the five plants wanted to move. I then dowsed to see where the plants wanted to go. Did any want to stay in the Silent Garden? YES, one got moved to a corner, and the other two were relocated to the Body Garden. I feel like I am a bit murky on my dowsing. I don't know if I am being answered or if the answer is just my opinion. I asked questions many times and sometimes I felt like the answers changed. I'll have to ask Sue to verify a few things, like the two marigold plants that wanted to stay where they were.

Then I weeded half of the empty weeded patch and I got an impressive sunburn. When I was in the garden, I was thinking about muscle-response testing and how I want to use it. It occurred to me that it focuses more on the questions that people don't stop to ask, and further, they don't stop to really feel the answer. They are simple questions. Do I want to do more garden work? Should I move this plant? No one ever asks these simple questions consciously. Everyone just seems to DO without really thinking. I should take the time to ask more.

Also, I need to practice saying prayers when I am joyful. It's always easy to say prayers when I need or want something or are if I ask for help. I would imagine that people wouldn't think to pray because they feel gratitude or are thankful or joyous.

We take happiness for granted, and then get upset when faced with adversity. Sounds a little spoiled to me. I am so tired, but happy. I'll say a short thank you prayer before sleep.

-Inée

About Diamond Gardens:

The first Diamond Gardens blossomed on Sue's farm in upstate New York early in the 1980's. As a mission to incorporate the element of spirit into daily living, Sue was determined to use gardening to help people enhance their perceptions. As an avid water dowser, she saw merit in incorporating muscle-response testing into this exercise. Diamond Gardening, named because each bed was the shape of a diamond, later became the classroom for awareness enhancement lessons.

She taught many Diamond Gardening techniques to local elementary schoolteachers interested in providing projects for classes. More than the intention of growing vegetables or cut flowers in a 12' x 12' plot, these Diamond Garden projects offered a way for children to gain autonomy. This autonomy resulted from providing food for one's self even if he was not grown up! Friendships with other Diamond gardeners built community. Sue wrote a thought-provoking workbook in 1993 called **Chain Of Diamonds** that became the basis for an international movement that energetically linked like-minded gardeners through their garden plots in countries around the world.

One intern from Germany wrote:

A Diamond Garden is a delightful place to open your heart. Using the garden as a metaphor you learn more about your self-nurturing patterns. Awareness increases as you recognize authentical reactions to a changing environment.

When I found myself noticing weeds and not the developing fruits I looked deeper inside to my critical tendencies. Seeking the joys of little changes was what I learned. Let nature enrich your inner emotional territory. I learned this too. Do this by mastering the art of merriment.

Another from Germany:

Since spending time in Todd, I became totally involved with Diamond Gardening. Now at the place I work that has a Senior Facility, we built raised Diamond Gardens. Oh they are so beautiful and the residents are happy even if they are in wheel chairs. They now can enjoy gardening pleasures.

CHAPTER NINE

BE YOURSELF AND ACT NATURALLY

The dictionary describes the verb – to personate – to represent in a manner in which you act out a part. Visitors at Growing Wheel who do not feel confident to be themselves often personate. This masks their ability to grow and develop their most creative and authentic selves.

Sue recalls that after a particularly demanding task in the hot sun she overheard an intern begin to complain about the suggestion to loosen up and act naturally. His memorable comment was, "Being yourself is a full time job!"

If you find yourself acting out the role of:

- Martyr
- Perfectionist
- Silent Critic
- Fear-filled Follower
- Sufferer
- Rebel
- Exhausted Helper in hopes to get praise

Ask yourself:

- Why do you believe that by adopting an identity
  you feel safer?
- Do you believe that if you assume an identity you will
  avoid feeling the deeper repressed pain?
- Do you believe that having an identity will provide you
  with a mask that deflects potential self-honesty by using
  the mask of a destructive character pattern that is easily
  identified by others?

If they accept this mask you will not have to search deeper to feel your authentic feelings.

Be yourself and act naturally. Act rightly. Allow your words and actions to be molded from the spirit of respect for yourself and others. This takes practice, as there may be some hidden destructive patterns that will want to be dissolved. This can happen gracefully and easily by feeling them, coping with them objectively and understanding these elements as something not healthy that can be changed within the surroundings of nature.

If you feel insecure, dowse for yourself:

- Am I forcing my interpretation of what others need
  onto myself to gain support?
- Am I receiving an overlay of mass-consciousness that
  is interfering with my personal desires?
- Is self-criticism causing me to misinterpret the situation?

If so, are any of these causing you to act in a way that you believe you should act?

Inée: Woke to a beautiful and fresh cloudy day. Said my Obligatory Prayer inside because the wooden deck outside was too wet. The neighbor and I planned to take Sue's vehicles to town to get them inspected and repaired as well as grocery shop. It was a very anxious atmosphere because Sue had many things to prepare before she left for her trip to Berlin. Everything felt rushed. Throughout the day I was realizing that I was critical. I was critical of the repair shop we went to — everything was junky and dirty and I really thought it needed renovation. I was very critical of my body (that day more-so than the average woman I suppose). I can't recall what else but I just remember that several times I had to acknowledge that I was being unnecessarily critical of my surroundings and myself.

I think self-criticism can stem from a lack of self-confidence. Perhaps I am always like this and it is more noticeable now that Sue pointed it out yesterday. Perhaps I am just extra critical in this phase of my life. It's funny that once someone points something out, you notice it more. I am slowly becoming more self-aware, and objective in my self-analysis. I am learning to accept myself for my imperfections and finding that there can be peace in knowing that one cannot be perfect in all areas of life. How much more stressful and agonizing would life be if you were constantly trying to be perfect in everything? Probably pretty miserable.

-Inée

I remember Sue said something like this:

"Use your skills of widened awareness to recognize the myriad of possibilities within any moment. Consider choosing the solution that sustains mutuality and fulfills your authentic needs. Until you are connected to this awareness, you will, most earnestly, engage in pseudo-solutions that mask the gifts available within your reach!"

This afternoon lesson was served simply while trimming branches by the bridge. Over the years she has taught multitudes of seminars to help students exchange generalizations for specifics.

Sue then explained about a clarified strength of mind:

"Notice the things you choose. Be aware of why you select certain things over others. Simple as it sounds, by practicing this awareness, you can actively influence the power of your decision-making ability! From your clarified strength of mind, your confidence can also grow. Why? You will be able to say, in clear translatable ways what you like and what you need. You become a confident judge. With your clear and critical awareness you build the respect of others who are drawn to your clarified strength of mind. Have you tried to enjoy something when you felt insecure? Most often it is not possible to experience enjoyment and insecurity at the same moment. Have you even been a host and asked a visitor what he wants to eat for lunch?

'Oh, I'm not sure. All your suggestions sound good.'

What responses might the host have?

- Shall I guess what they would like?
- Make what I like and take it on face value that she really has no preferences?
- Ask again and offer a more tantalizing description to get a response?

What would you do?"

Your enriched confidence is a product of your clarified strength of mind and will support the development of your choices, behaviors, skills, and viewpoints.

Inée: Over the past few days I have invited many new ideas into my mind. I have taken on the role of the student, absorbing as much information that Sue has to share as I can. I think it's rather motivating to see just how often I am critical of myself and my surroundings. I have become more aware than I ever was about how criticism can evolve and take different forms – like frustration and guilt.

I think that the source of criticism is inflexibility: the inability to accept and change with the changing conditions.

Slowly I began to melt my feelings of duality by altering the ideas in my mind that have previously been planted by society and the education system in general.

If I am not the "best" then that's okay.

From there I can learn and gain new insights that would allow me to progress much farther than if I were to believe that I was the "worst". There are times when I've greatly felt the need to be punished for doing something wrong or understanding something incorrectly. It is amazing that humans have learned so well that if they feel guilty, then they must have done something worthy of being punished.

Life is such a vast learning experience and we cannot afford the time or distress to punish ourselves when we feel the least bit guilty.

Instead we should be acknowledging our mistakes and taking a big step forward, instead of two steps backward. We evolve as we live so how can we ever expect to move forward if we keep pushing ourselves back? Soon I will begin to take the explorer's role in applying the knowledge I have gained and opening up my world to so many more opportunities.

-Inée

Sue mentioned that perfectionism and personal excellence are not the same. Perfectionism is so deeply ingrained that often a person can actually alienate himself from the moment's offerings by only focusing on perfectionism, as one believes perfection to be. This causes tension and then one sacrifices the experience of living in the true sense.

CHAPTER TEN

PERCEPTION ENHANCEMENT

Inée: Sue was enthusiastic as she explained the importance of appropriate awareness towards one's personal traits of flexibility and rigidity while developing sensitivities.

"You behave according to your perceptions of the world. Each person creates his own selective perceptions by using his senses. Your perceptions are most often determined by your wants and needs.

"Here is an example: When hunting for the most appropriate garden hat in the department store, the location of the perfume department may not be perceived (or remembered) even though its odor is quite noticeable to a passing shopper. Why? You are on a mission for the perfect hat. Perfume was not your want or need at that time. Your perceptions became selective. Hats. Hats. Hats.

"Many people who actively engage in cerebral activities of the day often do not realize that they have aching muscles, sore shoulders or lower back pain until after the workday is completed.

"The rigid attention to mental constructs eclipses the use of their five senses.

"Make a point to foster your flexibility. Practice by moving your attention in a rhythmic manner from one physical sense to another. Actively bring ambient information into focus, at least ten times an hour for practice.

The intern who enters from the west asked for an example of what he could do to move ambient information to the forefront of his attention.

"All types of information surround you. Bringing the specifics into your consciousness can be like a gentle dance. Here is an example as you requested.

"I am wearing moccasins and as I bow slightly and enter the department store to purchase the sun hat for the Diamond Garden, I feel the change of texture of the floor materials under my feet as I move from the sidewalk to the store tiles. I can feel my cotton shirt on my back as I bow and as a car passes behind me I judge its distance, size, and weight. I assess if it is a light or dark colored car from the reflections it bounces to the building's wall as it passes. I smell the air inside and determine simultaneously the temperature and the quality of the environment. Music or the high-pitched sounds of the alarm system are noted as well as my composure as I enter. I sense where the people are located as they are dense and complex patterns in a fairly unified setting of cloth, wood, plastic and metal. I use intuition to sense where I should go to find the item while reading the hanging signs in the direction that feels right.

"As I mentioned any rigidity to perceiving the actuality of the moment puts you in a cocoon. You can emerge from this shell. Use your senses. This brings you into the moment. If you a need to envelop yourself in security, focus your attention on the specifics of your wants or needs. From the target you can again widen your awareness of what is around you."

Sue has maintained local on-going Energy Awareness Classes since 1997. After learning about the seven major chakras and the electromagnetic fields, participants expand their abilities to nurture their innate gifts and strengthen their use of energetics in daily activities. A question about energy depletion when in new situations led to this lesson.

A class participant asked: Sometimes I think I give away my energy when I assist people at the front desk of the busy acupuncture office. When it gets hectic at work I think I take on other people's energy – how can I maintain my inner-balance?

"Energies are everywhere. I don't consider them as good or bad energies. People forget that there are also information-filled energies in objects and in places. Energies can be accessed through the Internet. Most of what people get bothered by is other people's thought form energy. Let's call this OPE. OPE is not negative or positive. This would be an oversimplified and a dualistic way of filing the multitudes of patterns within the incoming data.

Refine the feelings from OPE by building a language of sensations. Find words that match how you feel when you experience these energetic sensations. Once you can label these responses, you can communicate about them and describe the distinctions. It becomes a new language that is built upon recognition of these differences. Your sensory training can be widened to include the meta-sensory details. Your awareness of energies is built around your knowledge of the chakras and the electromagnetic fields that surround the body."

The Chakras and Electromagnetic Fields

The chakras are power centers of energy in your body. The word chakra is a Sanskrit word that means wheel.

(Ah, your organization is Growing Wheel – more dots are being connected.)

As your energy patterns become strengthened, seven major chakra vortex areas expand. The associated electromagnetic fields that surround your body strengthen and become resilient. The electromagnetic field, often called the aura, or the energy field, is packed with a myriad of energetic information.

"When I look at a person I can read this information in a similar way that you are reading these words. I don't always look at the colors around the body. This is because I don't focus on that frequency band of information. I am more interested in the stories that linger in the electromagnetic fields because these stories tell me what is not processed into the body's system."

One intern who approached from the north raised his inquiring hand:

"I understand the power of a person's energy field is based on the strength of the energy vortices called chakras. A person has seven major chakras. These vortices are force centers of rotating energy that receive and transmit information. Could you tell us more about each of these seven?"

"The seven major chakras are located on a central axis from the base of the spine to above the top of the head. The six major chakras correlate with specific languages of consciousness and evolution. The seventh chakra is your connection to the Universal Forces.

- **Chakra 1** is located at the root of the spine and relates to material things, the body, and the body's needs.
- **Chakra 2** is located in the pelvic region. It is concerned with things emotional, creative, and regenerative.
- **Chakra 3** is located in the solar plexus and is a vortex that aligns you with the world in which you live.
- **Chakra 4** is located in the heart center in the middle of the chest. It relates to the qualities of compassion, fairness, love, and equality.
- **Chakra 5** is located in the throat and aligns with one's communication skills, higher aspirations, and ideals.
- **Chakra 6** is located in the center of the forehead. It relates to conceptualizing ideas and carrying them out through the use of your mind and body's faculties.
- **Chakra 7** is at the crown of the head. This is central to your spiritual connection to the Universal Forces.

"This is an introduction. With more perception enhancement, you will be able to gracefully accept the power available through your chakras. This can be paralleled with the muscles of your physical body that can handle more complex movements when exercised. Later, I'll give a lesson on the balances and imbalances in the chakras."

Inée recalls after her second week as an intern at Growing Wheel: Filled with frustrations, from all that I have learned so far, I guess that these negative feelings had to do with externally generated, non-beneficial energy that was affecting my mood and energy field. I could have been picking up other people's energy (OPE) that was influencing the way I worked and what I interfaced with during the day.

Energy is all around us, and one must never underestimate its power. If I had known at the time how energy can alter how we operate in life. We must all be careful of our thoughts and emotions because they have the ability to carry all the way across the world and exercise their effect.

This has been an incredible journey so far and I have learned so much about the physics of energy. Now I have increased my awareness to such things that I could never have imagined were real, and I can continue with a new chapter in life that has more dimensions.

-Inée

Sue arrived at the House of Five Senses after completing a day of telephone consultations. Dressed in a bright colored blouse and sweeping skirt, she began a lesson about how to widen awareness about sensations one may feel if he has picked up externally generated non-beneficial energies.

"Encounters of the day may contain energetic components that are not noticed and difficult to discern. They may be disrupting your personal energetic signature.

"You may not notice OPE but you can notice such symptoms as:

- Headache
- Tiredness
- Partaking of food or drink not usually in your interest
- Sleeping patterns that are erratic
- Terrible and violent dreams, night terrors, dreams of dead bodies
- Yawning for no reason
- Motor skills that are not quite normal
- Anger for no reason
- Feeling separated from your surroundings, not feeling like you are in your body
- Ears feel congested or ring
- Pain in body for no reason

"These sensations can alert you to the notion that subtle energies are present and are disruptive to your energy system.

"Animals and people have their own personal energetic signature. This is an electromagnetic pattern. With good health, this configuration is protective and supportive.

"The energy signature can also be disrupted by such things as:

- Environmental influences such as empathic vibrations that are man-made/ confusing, power spots/power holes found in nature
- Technology
- OPE (other people's energy)
- Subtle energy residues that tend to be concentrated in products and thought forms based in these products

- Environs frequented by many for a single purpose, places of intense beliefs—like churches, meditation halls, and political or governmental buildings
- Historically traumatic or disruptive event locations

One curious student who wandered to the group to listen asked: How do I keep my unique signature when I am in unfamiliar settings that have distorted energy?

"I will use the example of a department store. People who visit a shopping mall surround themselves with the theme of selection. People go into a store and think, 'I like this, I don't like this, I saw this style, I like this color, I want, I desire. I want to know the cost. Would I look especially pretty in this?' This conglomerate of thought forms, plus the energies of the products that include how and where they were made, their vibrations while in transit, being touched by many, can all be quite confusing.

"It is possible to maintain your own unique signature that allows you to be less influenced to make needless purchases. By preparing yourself before entering the environment, you can strengthen your energetic immunity against those who have touched the products before you."

Sue explained that as she walks through the doorway of any building, or area that may cause her disruption, she performs a little — almost imperceptible — bow. This signals to her system to strengthen her own unique signature.

A student pointed out that in the Japanese culture it is common to place a cloth in the doorway of a building so when someone enters the space, they must bow. This reminds them of themselves and the respect for the moment. This simple gesture focuses them into the present.

The energetic process mentioned, to perform at the doorway of a store, for example, can be a practiced gesture that amplifies your energy field. As you move your attention from the top of your head into the ground, by a slight bow, you can discharge non-beneficial energies that may be clustering around you.

CHAPTER ELEVEN

SENSITIVITY PRACTICE

Sue shares recollections about practicing energy sensitivity in the woods:

"I started practicing ways to increase my perceptions when I was quite young. My father was an avid cave explorer and he loved to investigate innovative methods to enhance his love of caves. He became skilled as a dowser; after successfully finding the placements for the well for our homestead, our neighbors' homes, and his place of business, he started dowsing for caves! My sensitivity in this area started, I recall, when I was a very young child walking around the winter woods of upstate New York with a group of cavers. On most weekends, my parents and friends were searching for caverns to explore and survey.

"My father knelt down beside me and told me that my little feet could learn to tell if the earth below was solid or held cavities. He said that if I carefully moved along the rocky hillsides I could actually feel where the caves were. He explained that through feelings as well as topographic knowledge I might find a cave without an entrance. Then, he explained, the group would decide to dig down to open the cave or follow the geological signs and dig where there would be another potential entrance. How I tried that first day to feel the space below my tiny shoes. I could only feel textures. After thorough concentration while walking the ridges, I stopped and shouted to my father, 'Daddy! Here. A cave. I feel a space!'

He replied, 'Fine Dear. You now have the touch!' (Only later I learned that I had located a well-known and already mapped cave below my feet.)"

Inée: Woke up on the wrong side of the bed today for some reason. It was gray and rainy outside and I just felt so good to be cozy in bed. I don't remember when things started feeling uncomfortable for me, but I got to HoFS eventually and fed the excited pups, then drove up to Sue's place, HiTor, to feed the cat Ginger after feeding the HoFS cat Paloma. I went out to check the chickens and their water needed changing.

I think this was when I started getting irritable. As I was picking up the water bottle and the bowl, the rooster behaved aggressively, like he was going to rear up and spur me. To defend myself, and gain a little space, I held my foot in the air as he jumped up to attack. I yelped, but he didn't get me. I gathered the water bowl and the five-gallon bottle and steamed out.

This is when I started getting super angry. As I was taking the parts to the spigot to rinse and clean them, nothing seemed to cooperate with me – the bowl slipped, dirty water splashed on me, etc. When it seems that even inanimate objects won't even comply, I concluded that I was having a pretty frustrating day.

After the water bowl was clean, I returned it to the chicken pen. Rooster was aggressive. He got up to attack and I yelled "HEY!" and he stopped. I guess it made me mad that I was cleaning their water and feeding them, and then Rooster chooses to attack me.

I can't blame the animal though; it's natural for them. Perhaps I was agitated before I even got to the chickens and Rooster felt that energy and acted accordingly...animals know so much more than they let on. I planned to archive photos and cook today. I was prepping vegetables in between taking snapshots of the slides. After the dogs ran down the hill to bark at a car, and after I carried all three back uphill in my arms, I went back to archiving slides. The computer was off for some reason. pressed the power button and...nothing.

After trying unsuccessfully many times to turn on the machine, plugging it in various places, checking the cord and connection almost obsessively, panic set in.

I really wonder if Sue checked in on me from Berlin during this time and felt a frantic energy. How could this have happened? All I was able to think was that I DIDN'T DO ANYTHING WRONG.

The computer was completely dead. Dead as a doornail. I never did anything other than convert slides to Jpg so HOW COULD THIS HAPPEN? I went to Boone to see if the problem could be fixed. It's a motherboard issue, how horrible. I don't feel that I was too critical today, but it may have been disguised in my frustration this morning.

-Inée

"Hey everybody, would you like to try an energy experiment?" Sue sang out as she rounded HoFS wooden door threshold preceded by her three lively dogs.

This can be done with four or more people in a small group. Half the people in each group spend one minute conjuring up an agreed upon emotion. The others, not knowing what emotions are being sent, focus on their inner reactions to the others' silent transfers of emotions.

Unknowingly, for example, if you are surrounded by those who believe it is a dangerous world and send out the emotion of fear, you may make the conclusion (from the power of thoughts of others) that the world is a dangerous place. If the pervading emotion is of perfectionism, for example, one may pick up from the surrounding energies that any mistake will result in punishment.

The Energy Awareness group session was instrumental in increasing sensitivities of environments of places you go. You can feel happy inside and within minutes of entering a new place, you may feel yourself shift and feel ill tempered or angry, for example.

The group shared animated examples of experiences in new settings. After a short time, each remembered a time of being in an uncomfortable situation. Their attitudes altered and they sensed that they were somehow being influenced.

If you rent a DVD or video, the people who have watched it before you may have their residual energy lingering on it. Before you put the disk into your player, hold it in your hands and with directed will, restore the product to the filmmakers' original intent.

When you are in a place that makes you feel out of sorts, bring your attention into your solar plexus and let the energy there make you feel a bit warmer. Then say your name. This will fortify your personal energy system. The more you utilize the strength of your chakras, the more you build inner confidence.

"I assumed that all would be fine during my unplanned trip to Berlin, because we had no special visitors here and the routine would be rather easy for the interns. Those few days reminded me that I had not given them adequate training in the subtleties of the power of energetics before I left."

Inée: Rough morning today. I rushed to get ready and went to HoFS to find a note Sue left about things that need to be done sooner than later. I started on those tasks and afterward was waxing a large wooden Spanish door in HoFS, when Sue came in. I learned a very good lesson today. She came in quietly. I asked her how she was and in a normal tone of voice she said she was frustrated and angry – she felt that she was being disrespected on her own property. I was confused, nervous, and didn't understand quite what she meant.

We sat at the dining table and she started expressing her dissatisfactions. In a clear and logical manner, she stated that the neighbor and I were taking liberties, that we were overstepping our boundaries. We were treating the House of Five Senses like a hangout place instead of a sacred place to enhance and train our awarenesses and our perceptions. She didn't like that we were watching movies in there; that our neighbor was using things that belonged to Sue without her permission, and that we ate all the cookies Sue spent four hours to bake. She said the energy of HoFS was distorted and impure. It was the energy of clutter and many other indirect and negative frequencies.

She was scolding me and was upset about the state of the place. I apologized with teary eyes and she said it's not to be sorry. We then started to talk about her laptop and she was looking for files on it. She opened it and I plugged it into the outlet. She sat at the head of the table and I was to her right. I turned the laptop to face her so I could show her what I was doing. She leaned forward to see the screen better. She stood up and gestured at the fact that she was leaning so far over. She then yelled, "We're acting like children!" and started shoving the tables closer to the outlet so the cord could reach. She did this so swiftly that all the items on the table, the metal dragon centerpiece and my iMac mainly, rocked and swayed.

The dragon's heavy metal tail and claws knocked the computer screen and landed on the keyboard. I was too shocked and all I was able to do was help her move the tables silently. She paused for a moment to express how unhappy she was, and I quickly adjusted my computer so it would lie down and not fall off next time. She said she was about to move the tables again so I'd better watch out for my computer since it was the first thing I gave my attention to after she moved the tables. I was startled and scared and I had lots of heavy adrenaline running through me. Again I helped her move the wooden tables as silently and cooperatively as possible, picking up fallen chairs. I was quiet when she stopped, and felt fearful and guilty.

She arranged the chairs next to each other and sat down to

continue with the computer. I cautiously sat next to her to help. She asked what we were doing and when I began to tell her that we were searching for a file, I stuttered and stammered over my words. I was trying very desperately to hold back the crying but as soon as she acknowledged that I was upset, the tears flowed. I tried to suppress the tears while she told me it was good for me to experience this reaction as she apologized and asked if I was okay.

Sue said that in the future when I'm in school and studying to become a Naturopathic doctor, there may be people who want to smear me, who want to take me down. She said it is better that I am getting lessons about respect now with her, instead of later. She assured me that I am going to continue to change and evolve and also mentioned that I already look so different than the day when I got here, I can't imagine how though. We sat at the MacBook for a time and I helped her find a document.

She soon left to take care of a phone appointment and I went out the back door of HoFS, crouched down and cried. I felt like I still had residual anxiety from the sudden event and my adrenaline, and that I needed to express it to feel relief. If I didn't let myself truly feel the tension inside, I'm sure I would have been quite uncomfortable the rest of the day. It's very beneficial to not only let yourself feel your real emotions, but also to understand and accept them. Although I felt rather small and guilty at the time, I knew it was healthy to allow these feelings to freely drop from me in this moment of emotion. I cried very briefly and felt significantly better, then continued with my duties.

After Sue finished her phone appointment she returned to HoFS at around 5pm. Things seemed to be a lot calmer.

We talked about trust and that it comes in three phases: Blanket trust (I trust that everyone I meet will be nice to me), Evidential trust (I won't believe this is organic until I have the proof), and Flexible trust (I can trust him to cook a fabulous meal, but not to organize an event). The Blanket trust is a childlike trust, one trusts in everything. The Evidential trust is adolescent, skeptical and rebellious, or experimental. Flexible trust is the mature form of trust in that it also includes one's intuition, deductive reasoning, and experience.

Then it was time for Perception Class tonight. I asked her in the car on the way if car sickness is an ailment that can be corrected. She said that it can and that I could practice my dowsing to check if the problem is in my cellular memory or if it is an issue of the physical anatomy in the membrane within my ears. In class we talked about the importance of hydration and dowsing: water whets the hemoglobin, which expands the blood and activates the autonomic nervous system.

The dowsing system is an intangible entity. We can heal ourselves using the dowsing system if it is appropriate. In this class we also learned about the Twelve Universal Principles. The Principles are virtues like Vibration, Order, Creativity, Congruency, Unity, and Attraction. Each person has the potential (or ability) to have twelve basic principles running through the body. We did an exercise to dowse how many of the Principles we had currently running at their optimal levels.

First, we dowsed to make sure that our dowsing was 100% accurately aligned with truth. YES.

Then we asked about how many Principles were utilized by our system without deviation. I had twelve, the other two ladies had twelve and more than twelve, and another student had four. He dowsed to see if he has ever had all twelve running, and it was a NO. Sue helped him dowse to find the cause: emotional, spiritual, or mental? NO. Environmental? YES. Is it diet, geopathic, season, social? NO. Physical? YES. Organs? YES. Sue narrowed down to the spleen and liver while he dowsed.

She told him to heal using the power of the dowsing system and that his body will rock forward when the work is done. He experienced many autonomic reactions like shivering and twitching (he is well attuned to being connected with this energy) and then his body rocked forward several times. After doing so with both organs, he dowsed again to see if all twelve Principles were running. YES. Awesome. Sue said he'd feel differently now since he's never had twelve functioning fully in his system.

I saw our young neighbor making cookies in the House of Five Senses with her boyfriend. They were baking muffins. I told her that we need to be more careful not to treat this place like a hangout, and that we need to be more mindful of the delicate energies at play here.

-Inée

Chapter Twelve

MY CHAKRAS

Inée: Today after I weeded almost the whole garden patch near the pond and erected an old iron gate as a trellis, I compared my chakras to the chakra book that Sue lent me to read. From Sue's perspective, my chakras are in their growth stages with the full potential being at 10. I am still at the growing stage of 2 for my heart chakra. I don't know why exactly. Heart chakra's vibration is about unconditional loving, self-love, and love for life. It also deals with the feelings of worthiness to give and receive love, embracing life. Is it low because I am afraid to love so freely?

If I show everyone such love (platonic or compassionate love), then it is likely that some will perceive this as romantic love and try to pursue me. If this happens and I cannot return those romantic feelings, it usually results in hurt feelings — something I never want to cause. Maybe that sounds egotistical but it has happened several times in my life and I want to avoid that. Maybe my heart chakra's current rating is low because I was quite hurt in my last relationship and I fear to open up to others in such a way. Perhaps I am just trying to be careful and guarded so people don't develop the romantic affection for me that I cannot return.

I have no idea why my crown chakra is currently registering so low. The crown chakra deals with spiritual understanding and an acknowledgement and gratitude of a higher power. The book describes that a dysfunctional crown chakra has a negative attitude of egotism. Since my crown chakra was rated at a 1, I really wonder if it means I am egotistical, or selfish, or spiritually ignorant. I feel quit the opposite. I pray genuinely everyday, I strive to be humble and in alignment with God's will, and I hold God and my Faith with the utmost reverence. I don't fully understand this chakra...

-Inée

Sue explained that chakras are quite fluid and they open and close in various settings. The flexibility of a chakra is important to cultivate. When people interact, their chakras, and the associated energy fields meld and energetic bonds can form. These bonds can be short or long-term energy contracts. When people come together and are comfortable and aligned, the energy fields merge and assimilate. When the interaction is completed, each returns to his or her unique pattern without taking any of another's energy or leaving anything behind. If a person's chakra is not at its full functioning form, it may be due to a melding with others who don't share the same tuning. This may disrupt your personal frequency. It is not bad. You learned that nothing is good or bad. It signals that you can be more flexible to maintain a correlated energy contract. Using your resiliency, you can return to your individual pattern when appropriate.

Inée inquires: I would like to know more about the chakra system. Can you tell me about each chakra and the correlated energy contracts you spoke about?

"In the Hindu tradition, each chakra is connected to a color, a sound, a nerve plexus, and a glandular system. It is true that the more one connects to her own energy system, the more she can align with timeless qualities that are held in the collective knowledge accumulated about the chakras. Take the time to learn where these chakras are located. When you have memorized each chakra's location and the associated color you can research each chakra's Sanskrit name, its sound, geometric shape and deities that relate to each one."

Chakra 1 | RED
The first chakra, or root chakra, is the center of the physical self and the material world. It is associated with the element of earth and has been called the area of manifestation. It represents the pure urge to live and be health-filled. Located between your legs, its funnel-like shape opens downward toward the earth and vibrates as the color red. If this chakra is out of balance, there may be egotistic, greedy, or indiscriminating erotic energies that may cause discord to your operating system.

Chakra 2 | ORANGE
The second chakra, located in the pelvic region, controls the sexual and reproductive areas as well as the power of one's creative activities and flexibility in all situations. In consciousness, this center represents the concentration of pain and pleasure that is acted upon through conditioning or discipline. Often called the seat of personal desires, a person can enact negative or positive emotional choices

from this area of the subtle energy body. The water element, associated with this chakra can be used in many positive ways. The associated color is orange. With directed attention one can align this creative area with the Universal Principles and a focus on positive desires. If this chakra is out of balance, resentfulness, distrust, oversensitivity and shyness may cause discord.

Chakra 3 | YELLOW

In consciousness, the third chakra relates to one's inner authority as well as intellect and the connection to the higher astral and mental planes. It is located in the solar plexus. As one aligns with the elements of his third chakra, he will strengthen the boundaries of his energetic territory. The element is fire. From the disciplined power available from this chakra, one's fire can burn in a controlled and sustained manner. The associated color is yellow. If this chakra is out of balance, a lack of confidence, poor digestion, confusion, or a fear of being alone may become apparent.

Chakra 4 | GREEN

In consciousness, this chakra, located in the center of the sternum in the area of the heart, has been thought of as the seat of the human soul. The fourth major chakra acts as a bridge from the lower three chakras to the higher realms. Its color is green. "When the heart chakra opens", I was once told, "it feels like a loaf of warm bread just out of the oven placed in front of your chest." For some reason, I have never forgotten that. If this chakra is out of balance, indecisiveness, a fear of getting hurt, undeserving beliefs about love, and/or terrified feelings of rejection may cause discord.

Chakra 5 | SKY BLUE
The fifth chakra is located in the throat and works with the power of the fourth chakra and rules the functions of the lungs as well as all aspects of respiration. In consciousness, this chakra relates to the imagination, one's orientation to society and higher desires. This center relates to higher desires. It has been called the etheric center, or akashic center, as well as the seat of the angelic soul. If this chakra gets out of balance, unreliability, weakness, selfishness, deviousness, strategic manipulation, and inaudibility that may cause discord to others.

Chakra 6 | INDIGO
As the center of spiritual perception and knowledge, the sixth chakra controls the pineal gland. It is located in the forehead area and is connected to both the sympathetic and parasympathetic nervous system. Strengthen this part of your subtle energy body to enrich your ideas with the capacity to clearly carry out your thoughts with integrity and honor. If this chakra is out of balance, non-assertiveness, fear of success and lack of discipline may cause discord.

Chakra 7 | THE PRISM COLORS / WHITE
The area that expands like a crown, located at the top of the head, allows the integration of one's total personality with life and the spiritual aspects of mankind. Sue sees this area as a multi-faceted prism of lights filled with vignettes of images and stories. If this chakra is out of balance it may cause one to seek the vibrations from another's spiritual energy patterns. (This feels like being pulled down to rational and self-destructive thoughts that are opposite to exalted feelings one gets from the crown chakra.)

CHAPTER THIRTEEN

PURPOSE OF LIFE

Sue believes that it is appropriate to ponder the age-old question about the purpose of life. Her teachings reflect that a purpose of life is to fulfill our authentic needs. This occurs when one builds and maintains an accurate filing system on all levels of consciousness. Then energies are used, not to protect the body defensively in a way that causes tension, but directs energies towards creative and progressing solutions that continue the evolution of civilization in an inspired manner that aligns with timeless traditions.

"What is your belief about the purpose of life?" Sue asked one cloudless morning by the garden.

A quiet intern, after pondering this philosophical question, answered easily:

The purpose of life is to practice elaboration and on-going modification. These activities can be categorized into:

- Directed personal work to weed out inner inconsistencies inside that show up in relationships and in business.
- Inner purification: some examples are like meditation and yoga—to keep the mind, spirit, and body fit.

Some interns agreed that the purpose of life is to amplify the center of truth within.

Two others were sure that the purpose of life is to find love and share it every day.

Some interns mentioned that the purpose of life is to live in a secure and comfortable way without conflict – and to keep people happy.

One intern was convinced that no person's purpose of life is to suffer, be alone or struggle.

Another intern deliberated until last. She spoke slowly.

"I think that the purpose of life is to assess things. Like:

- What are your pleasures and your thoughts?
- What do you like to talk about with others?
- What types of efforts take your interest?
- What actions keep you involved?
- What are your ethical and moral convictions?
- What are you aware of?"

Sue concluded that whatever your life purpose may be, it is advantageous to systematically release:

- False conclusions
- Erroneous beliefs
- Contradictory attitudes and
- Misfiled input

to fulfill your life purpose.

One studious intern made a chart to use with muscle-response testing to help her discover entry points of study:

Thinking
- Understanding
- Reasoning
- Concentration
- Wisdom

Feeling
- Mindfulness
- Sentiments
- Concentration
- Direct Knowing
- Intuition

Reacting
- Desires
- Integrities
- Communication
- Action

Willing
- Determination
- Courage
- Tenacity
- Steadfastness
- Responsible Acceptance

How can I fulfill my authentic needs?

• Surroundings
• Behavior patterns
• Skills
• Abilities
• Values
• Viewpoints
• Identity

Would my personal development be expanded by:

• Penetrating into new realms (by trying new things; exhibiting new behaviors)?
• Giving forth from my inner resources (exploring my potentials)?
• Eliminating walls of separation (sharing with others in new ways)?
• Courage and strength (daring to make mistakes)?
• Actively motivating myself past comfort zones to achieve goals (stretching my horizons)?

Would you benefit from strengthening your chakras by bringing more awarenesses to:

• Thinking?
• Feeling?
• Reacting?
• Willing?
• Being?

Do you withhold your ability to use your creative strength?

If so, is this due to inner rigidity in the topic areas of:

- Thinking?
- Feeling?
- Reacting?
- Willing?
- Being?

Does this rigidity lead you to:

- A tendency toward burnout?
- Defenses that stifle your creativity?
- A refusal to adequately provide support for those you are with?
- Isolate or separate from the actuality of the present situation?
- Other

Take time to become your own inner counselor. Use your conscious mind to make a list of questions and then use muscle-response testing to check if all aspects inside are working in alliance.

We have learned that innermost strengths and perceptions cannot function as long as they are encased in the pseudo-protective shell of isolation. Intimacy is often misunderstood and thus avoided.

The dictionary definition of intimacy lists a sexual relationship in the place after close acquaintance, personal close friend and confidant. If you feel intimacy and sexuality are synonymous, your authentic adult needs may be more difficult to fulfill.

At Growing Wheel we care deeply about clear and honest associations on our campus. Interns seek intimacy in the form of close acquaintances, personal close friends, and confidants. They are volunteers. They want the same things traditional employees want. A study in 1992 detected that of the hundreds of people surveyed, employees wanted:

- Appreciation for their work
- The feeling of being kept up on business plans
- Help with personal problems
- Job security
- Compensation for effort
- Interesting work
- Comfortable working conditions and
- Tactful discipline

Taking a working definition of intimacy, people, whether paid or not, seek to fulfill authentic needs: to express themselves, feel that they make a meaningful contribution, are appreciated, and feeling camaraderie while getting to the goal.

Appreciation and love are sometimes confused and this causes problems with intimacy. Intimacy that grows from explorations helps colleagues to build successes that open up new emotional pathways.

Sue likes to touch this topic carefully with grace. It is a topic that enables people to gain confidence. The way she teaches about intimacy is through the approach that people may choose not to engage in building close and caring relationships because of imagined disappointment. Imagined disappointment leads to inner frustration and passive withdrawal.

If there is a false understanding about the definition of intimacy — meaning only sexual association, people will create pseudo-boundaries. Pseudo-boundaries block the communication possibilities between people with similar dispositions. Energetically this can be described as a push/pull energy that is very confusing to all participants. It is the seesaw effect between submissiveness and distorted self-assertion.

In an objective way, sense if you have any false conclusions in your:

• Thinking
• Feeling
• Reacting
• Willing

that interfere with positive and health-filled intimacy with others.

Use your skills of dowsing to find and remove or neutralize those false conclusions from your system.

CHAPTER FOURTEEN

APPRECIATION AND LOVE

Most people on the planet have heard at least one time, the old Beatles' song, "All You Need Is Love."

"You would have to be a potato if you didn't know that song." Inée kidded.

The words are as fresh today as when it was first made popular.

Perhaps if any leader was to list two most important things to share – all you need is love. All you need is to share appreciation. Simple as it seems, in the decades of taking the leadership role, I have observed it is only when workers can tolerate the possibility of receiving appreciation, that they can find fulfillment.

If a person does not know how to appreciate himself, he will not be able to accept appreciation from others. He has become numb to his authentic need for love, which hampers his self-expression and his appreciation for others.

Self-expression at Growing Wheel is part of the curriculum. In the evenings, people gather at the puppet stage, recycled from a feature film set, and the adjacent proscenium arched stage. Homemade artistic videos of personal viewpoints, outrageous puppet antics, and playful drama expand self-expression for all who care to play. By the end of the third act, much appreciation and love abounds.

Can you discern the difference between the meaning of appreciation and love? Many people feel that if they do something wrong, then they will not be loved. Unconditional love does not discriminate as to whether you did something that you considered right or wrong. Unconditional love is without limitations, and free of dualism. Appreciation is different. It relates to the recognition of a person's qualities or aptitudes. Love and appreciation of self and others are important no matter what type of work you are involved in.

Inée: When I engage in service or other volunteer work, mutual benefit for a higher purpose naturally occurs. It is through service that I learn about myself in a different manner than if I were to receive compensation for my efforts. In service, I am dedicating my time and my resources – myself – to whatever project I endeavor to complete.

Because of the selfless nature of volunteer work, I am able to more clearly and purely discern nuances in my personality and how my mind works. Am I patient when I expect to receive acknowledgement for work I have done and do not get instant recognition? With service and the act of being selfless, we can more directly access the higher virtues of self, and attain their beautiful qualities.

Greed, ego, superiority, rewards, and competition are no longer concerns. I can achieve goals and complete projects just for the sake of gaining the accomplishment; not because I want to be recognized for my skill, paid for my efforts, or win the prize. By being involved in something bigger than yourself, while forgetting yourself, you make contributions of magnanimous proportion to not only your inner being, but you positively affect everything around you.

The uncomplicated act of volunteer service opens doors for you to run out into the orchards of virtuous fruit and take your pick of juicy qualities like patience, appreciation, humility, trustworthiness, and certitude. I look forward to sharing the spiritual gifts I find along the path winding through my life.

-Inée

CHAPTER FIFTEEN

DREAM SIGNALS

Inée: Sue, how could you tell that your stained glass window dream was not just…well, a dream?

"Now that you are familiar with the major chakra system, you will find a simple way to remember categories I defined to help you with dream interpretation. I created a system to correlate the seven types of dreams with the activities that are common with the chakras. When you find out through muscle-response testing which category of dream you had, you can use the characteristics of the chakra and the power in that chakra to help you work with the information contained."

Inée: That's intense, could you give me some more background on dreaming?

"A dream is a brain activity that occurs while you are sleeping. It is a cognitive experience that is available to both humans and animals. You can alter experiences while engaged in dreaming. This can be done by expanding your awarenesses of the four stages of sleep and their energetic connections."

Some dreams can predict the future. Some dreams are mystical and tap into broader consciousness with others who are telepathic.

Starry-eyed Inée eagerly asked: How can you tell what happened in a dream once you wake up?

Psychologists, scientists, poets, philosophers and artists have long used dreams as a source for their deeper understanding about the world. Investigation I have done into dreams directed me toward two distinct areas. This is the core of this lesson.

- **Area One** to gain the ability to discern what type of dream you remembered.
- **Area Two** to learn what to do after discovering what category your dreams fit into.

In the past months I completed some independent research to further help those interested in tracking and organizing this elusive yet highly important cognitive experience. Although scientists have not yet been able to fully explain the dreaming process, it is clear that people and animals dream when asleep.

Dreams help our brains to grow by exciting and stimulating neurons. Dreams also help us to file the myriad of impressions we take in during the day. There are four stages of sleep that have been carefully identified:

LEVELS OF SLEEP

- **Stage 1:** if not disturbed, one will sink into the next stage

- **Stage 2:** images appear but plots are not usually evident
- **Stage 3:** muscles relax and heart rate slows. Blood pressure falls and breathing becomes even and steady.
- **Stage 4:** this is the stage where dreams occur. If you are awakened while in this state you will probably remember your dreams. In an average night's sleep you may reach this stage 3-5 times. Sometimes you may maintain this level for up to 45 minutes.

Studies have shown that people, who are upset or show signs of despair, seem to dream more than those who are happy. During the dreaming state, unprocessed emotions are sorted to remove their disturbing aspects. This type of sleep has been labeled paradoxical sleep because it does not create rest. Often, anti-depressants and other sleeping aids reduce the ability for one to reach the fourth level of sleep. Thus the inner filing system is not able to reduce the agitation and anxiety by processing the emotions.

I designed a chart to help you to identify the type of experiences you had while you were asleep. With focused practice you may even be able to expand your experience to lucid dreams from which gain more understanding while in the sleeping state.

Here is an outline to help you feel secure when a dream is particularly alarming or disquieting.

Your first target is to determine the type of dream you had by muscle testing. And then from there, find how you can productively use this information in a beneficial and appropriate manner. Innermost sincerity is an important factor in achieving success by not embellishing the contents of your dreams.

DREAM SIGNALS

Here are some suggestions:

When you first open your eyes after sleeping, do not move your body's position. This helps you to better recall your dream. Did a person, location, action, quest, or emotion come to your mind? If so, follow the recollections in a quiet and objective manner. It is important that you do not try to interpret the meaning of these elements. Evoke the memoires in a passive and supportive way. After you remember one dream, let your mind become blank and allow another dream to surface. If it does, follow the contents of this dream in the same manner. When you feel satisfied that your important dreams have been recalled, stretch, arise and jot down your findings. Place the date on the paper. The more often you practice your personal dream collection time, the easier it will be to gain the nuances of what transpires while you are sleeping.

Don't worry if you believe that you NEVER dream or cannot remember your dreams. Practice these steps for a few nights and let your subconscious have a chance to communicate with your inner willingness. Perhaps then you will gain insights.

Types of Dreams

1 – Rest. Physical rejuvenation.
2 – Inner psychological work. Filing of personal and emotional experiences during sleep.
3 – Communication with others. Living or not living. Working out something for the betterment of both.
4 – Non-beneficial rapport with others. Living or not living. This can be cleared during your waking state using the steps below.

5 – Precognition dreams. Something that is dreamed
will manifest.

6 – Inspiration from dreams. Something that is dreamed is
useful and has a positive purpose in your daily life.

7 – Spiritual revelation in dreams.

Inée: This is fascinating! Can you tell me more about how to
proceed?

What type of dream did you have?

1 | Rest:

Physical and mental rejuvenation dreams are usually
characterized by activities that seem pleasant and do not hold
anxiety-producing subject matter. An example: you dreamed
about a white kitten with a pink bow. The cat jumped out of a
basket licked itself on the porch and then laid down in the sun.
If you remember a dream such as this that feels neutral, there
is no need to search for a deeper interpretation.

2 | Inner psychological work:

Dreams of this type are the result of the brain's capacity to
file personal experiences during your sleeping time. You may
remember segments of this activity when you awaken. It is
natural and supportive to do inner psychological work while
asleep.

3 | Communication with others:

Type three dreams include a person or animal that is living or not living. While your conscious mind is at rest, you are working out something for betterment of all concerned.

Please note that not every dream about your deceased grandmother, for example, fits into this category. There may be a chance that during the day you used Grandma's teacup and her memory went into the recesses of your mind. A dream about her would be better placed in type 2. Usually type 3 dreams make you feel refreshed and at peace. Often you do not remember the course of events that took place.

4 | Non-beneficial rapport:

When you review type 4 dreams you may feel uncomfortable. After you piece together the action in your dream you may find that the contents make you feel less than cheery. The environments may seem gloomy and you may feel tense when you review the parts. The non-beneficial rapport with others, living or not living, can be cleared during your waking state using the method outlined below:

1. Determine that your dream is a type 4 dream.

2. Once assessed, bring your attention to the solar plexus area of your body

3. Speaking from your heart verbalize the following:

"You and I are in a non-productive contract. I believe you are protecting yourself against the unknown and have aligned with me. I do not want to

be in a contract with you. You have manifested destructive patterns that are affecting my consciousness. This distortion is a potent energy that is causing me to lose my flexibility and personal freedom. You hold a false belief that you can connect with me without my permission. You are in deviation of Universal Law if you subversively try to control me. You are defending yourself with a self-devised view of reality. You are not in danger. Move to your next level of development. Do not reconnect with me. This is dishonoring me as well as yourself. You are responding to false conclusions. Aligned with Universal Power, I say, you will leave now."

4. Bring your attention to your feet and if you feel an autonomic release in your body, breathe rhythmically until you feel lighter and back to your own style.

5 | Precognition Dreams:

Precognition means that you have access to information of something that will occur in the future. The elements of your dreams will probably manifest unless you intervene in some manner. For many this is common. For others, precognitive dreams become alarming. Once you can clearly distinguish between the type 2 dreams and these, you will be able to use your free will to shift the future using creative solutions aligned with the topic of the dream. It is my belief that you are given this information for a purpose. Take the responsibility as one would in the waking state. Your ethical and moral development will assist you.

6 | Inspiration from dreams:

Many inventors, Thomas Edison, for example, would take short naps during the day and night when working on a new innovation. Many times the answer would come forth in less than a half-hour. When you dream of something special and it is something not known to you, check if what was dreamed is useful and has a positive purpose in your life or in the lives of those around you.

7 | Spiritual revelation in dreams:

Once you have experienced a type 7 dream you will always be able to identify them. There is an overwhelming sense of gratitude and interconnectedness that is retained in your system long after you begin your day.

Dreams are a rich source of information. When you create systematized order to assist your dream patterns you are able to clearly understand the language of your dreams. The interpretation of your dreams follows the qualities of the seven major chakras. By reading each of the dream descriptions you can establish a congruent system that could be called upon when you awaken and review your dreams.

Dream Descriptions:

• Dreams in categories 1 and 2 relate to ordinary functions of rest and rejuvenation. Chakra 1 relates to the physical body and health. Chakra 2 relates to your creative self.
• Category 3 relates to energetic connections that emerged while asleep and are beneficial to all concerned. Chakra 3 relates to your relationship to the world.
• Category 4 shows unsolicited connections that are non-beneficial and cause distress. Chakra 4 relates to the heart.
• Category 5 is precognitive and offers you the opportunity

to use your creativity to choose how to deal with the accurate information. Chakra 5 is associated with higher communication.

- Category 6 dreams are inspirational. Chakra 6 relates to the constructs of ideas and imagination. The information received from a type 6 dream can be used in your daily life.
- Category 7 dreams are a gift from the spiritual realms. Chakra 7 relates to the connection to the spiritual realms. Hold on to these dreams, they are uplifting and filled with support.

Inée: How do you suggest I create a dream journal of these insights?

In your dream journal, always make sure to include the date and the content of the dream. From there you can look at the dream categories and discern which category it fits under. Try to recall the dream in as much detail as possible so that later you can start to notice patterns and other recurring themes.

"Dreams seem to be more intense during one's stay at Growing Wheel, as all of the sleeping places are located around the 32 paths of the Kabbalah. The Kabbalah is a Hebrew term meaning to receive. It has a long spiritual heritage from the first century when the Yetzirah (meaning formation) continued the oral tradition through to the 13th century in Spain when a treatise entitled Zohar (meaning splendor) appeared and spread the word and teachings about the Tree of Life. Each of the paths has attributes and all of these qualities collaborate for those who stay here. Like a homeopathic frequency, they can rebalance, support, and widen awareness of how to include pleasures to enhance the flow of life. In times of intolerance or instability, dreams and the frequencies of the Kabbalah aid interns to strengthen their inner virtues."

Inée: I recall my beginning at Growing Wheel: First night at Growing Wheel in Todd. It is so nice to be at this place. When I got here, Sue took me all around the property and showed me all the potential places I could stay, none of which have electricity.

After all that, I decided that I wanted to stay in the place that she had originally intended for me. I am staying in the Garden Hut and it is pretty central in the facility. There is no electricity in here, but tomorrow I can dig a small line from the Sundown Theatre to the hut and get power. Maybe I won't use it much other than a little non-candle lighting and to charge my phone.

It'll be good to be disconnected from my computer and not have any Facebook, Internet, movies, etc. I will have more time to read books and truly take in more nature and healing energy. She told me that this particular cabin had a feminine energy, is oriented for success, and deals with moral ethics, and authenticity of self.

Then Sue and I went to change the light bulb near the outdoor shower. I told her that I don't mind just showering before it got dark, but she made a point that one should be careful of decisions like this. If one only takes a shower during the day because the light bulb needed to be changed, then does this mean that when it gets dark, that it's too late to shower?

She said "change a light bulb, change your life".

I guess the overall meaning is that we shouldn't just change the way we live simply because it seems more convenient than fixing the problem.

We should live with the intent of purpose, efficiency – necessity. If something is broken, fix it. It's a very useful and applicable lesson: not to take the convenient path, but to take the path that is necessary and efficient.

Unfortunately, after many switches were flipped, the new light bulb was unsuccessful. Sue has been very accommodating – she made a spaghetti squash casserole and invited the neighbor to eat with us. She is a lovely young girl of 20 who takes people on kayak, canoe, and tubing adventures down the river for her job. It was a delicious meal and I was so hungry for something hot.

Sue told me that often times things that people have repressed start to emerge and be uncovered after spending about a week here. Whatever my negative energies may be I look forward to seeing them expressed and then come into balance. I can't imagine what is going to happen. And now I am having déjà vu that I am writing by candlelight in a cabin on Sue's property... how strange.

-Inée

CHAPTER SIXTEEN

BITS AND PIECES
TO SHARE

Here is a paper written by a student after a summer visit to Todd, NC:

The learning arena of 100 acres granted me a free and open opportunity to look deeper into my desires and reactions. It became a microcosm of awareness. These experiences were clear metaphoric teaching tools. I gained a stronger clarity about my personal desires. I learned that noble motives might contain selfish desires. It is not possible to force your feelings away! It is common to mask reality. This process leads to self-deception. Often you may get vague feelings of "confusion". This may signal that you are suppressing your conflicting desires. I do not believe that it is possible to override "lesser or hidden desires". I have observed that hidden desires are the force behind disharmonies, disappointments, conflicts, and many illnesses. The experience at Growing Wheel gave me the opportunity to stretch to new behavior using creative endeavors as the liberating experience for everybody involved.

Our goal was to increase our perceptions in a way that made us more creative and integrity filled. Sue gave us opportunities to feel nobler out of a free spirit of giving and taking. I did not know how selfish I was until I spent time at Growing Wheel.

I learned that self-knowledge is a prerequisite to hold and sustain love and self-knowledge is the necessary foundation for true service to others. Once you are aware of your own emotional needs there is no confusion as to transference of "service to others" of what is personally desired within one's self.

Emotions are potent areas to enhance awareness. Any protective mechanisms color our emotional experience. Our convictions, opinions and beliefs that are not fortified by a clear emotional currentare weak and distorted. To succeed as a health professional it is necessary to understand your emotions and gain a clear picture of what type of emotional force is leading you. I gained years of experiences in this wonderfully planned intensive experience. I would do it again.

The questions that were most important for me came from the handout that Sue left in my cabin. I include it here for others to use. How these questions changed my life! I kept this handout as it helped me gain insights about intimacy with others:

Questions for Reflection:

Do you hold emotional rigidity keeping you from understanding your own emotional style?

Do you judge others due to unprocessed emotions inside yourself that keep you from feeling confidant and secure? If so, is it appropriate to find and release what is:

- Blocked?
- Hindered?
- Prohibited?
- Sublimated?
- Numbed?
- In resistance to Truth?

Do you recognize when others use defense techniques such as:

- Denial?
- Blame?
- Withholding?
- Excusing?
- Dodging?
- Attacking?
- Minimizing?
- Generalizing?
- Self-rejection?

If not, is this due to areas yet unprocessed within yourself?

Is this defensive posture a protection against imagined pain or fear?

Do you repress anger because admitting that you feel anger may make you feel unsafe or out of control?

If so, do you also hold hidden feelings of:

- Resentment?
- Self-pity?
- Stress?
- Anxiety?

- Unhappiness
- Sorrow?
- Lack of concentration or confusion?
- Physical discomfort or pain?

If so, can you find more creative ways to:
- Feel safe and express your anger appropriately?
- Identify inner hurt feelings that underlie the anger?
- Understand disappointments within yourself and
  with others?
- Set limits for yourself so you feel satisfied rather than
  frustrated or angry?
- Reduce your stressfulness by sharing responsibilities?
- Sleep if you are tired?
- Eat if you are hungry?
- Be honest in a loving manner?
- Be loyal to yourself?
- Seek inner approval rather than the approval from others?

Do you understand that an action, a thought, an attitude or a conclusion is not good or bad?

On all levels of consciousness do you believe that the values of an action, thought, or attitude are motivated by love? If not, are they motivated by fear, arrogance, or false authority?

Do you have a hidden numbness that keeps you from expansion and development?

If so, is it due to an inability to:
- Identify your feelings?
- Express your authentic feelings?

- Experience intimacy?
- Experience and share your true self?
- Express your needs to others?

Do you isolate creative parts of yourself due to a fear of:
- Rejection?
- Judgment?
- Separation?
- A sense that you are not perfect?

Do you hold a hidden need to be excessively responsible?

If so, do you also:
- Take each task of life extremely seriously?
- Remain inflexible?
- Have false pride?
- Manipulate others?
- Assume too much responsibility for others?
- Become perfectionistic?

Would it be helpful for you to keep a journal to help widen your awarenesses of your feelings and sensations?

CONCLUSION

Growing Wheel's Intern Program is a microcosm of experiences people have in their daily lives. While interacting with people, animals, or in nature energies are an important component of the experience. Usually people cannot take the time to express their authentic feelings or their primal insights about the role of energetics. Interns are granted a chance to explore their perceptions in a carefully tuned environment that assists each helper to focus attention on the principles of cause and effect, attraction, concord, compensation, circulation, resiliency, vibration, and balance. Time devoted to awareness enhancement sets a tone for building enriching experiences after the season at Growing Wheel is over.

CHAPTER SEVENTEEN

FURTHER TRAINING
FUNDAMENTALS OF BODY ENERGETICS
TRAINING PROGRAM

Newly revised and thoroughly updated for this season is a comprehensive course about the use of your energy system to enhance dynamics during communication. It is intended for both serious-minded health practitioners and those with busy lifestyles who yearn for a deeper understanding of the power of energetics in daily interactions.

The Fundamentals of Body Energetics Training Program offers proficiency within five platform areas. An accompanying book *Platforms of Evolution* is a companion to the seminar study. This training differs from the information that has been taught to students of the Fields of Understanding School of Principled Consciousness also founded by Sue Gurnee. Students participating in the Fundamentals of Body Energetics Training do not focus on creating an individual project as students do in the year-long school.

The course includes the topics:
• Chakras and your energy body
• Energetic connections with others
• Energies are in everything
• Toxic Energy
• Basic Skills to deal with energies
• Energy alignments
• Giving and receiving energies
• Clarity
• Accountability
• Support
• Appreciation
• Trust
• Unity
• Growth, Liberation, Strength
• Desires, Truth, Manifestation
• Sensibility, Practicality, Mastery
• Muscle-Response testing

Sample **Platforms of Evolution** chapters include the topics:
• How energy attacks happen
• How to disconnect from others
• Ways to clean your aura daily

Any students who are currently enrolled in the Fields of Understanding's School of Principled Consciousness may participate in the Fundamentals of Body Energetics Training Course.

Interested students meet for four days, two times a year at varied locations. To help hasten the evolutional process, workbooks with lessons in English and German are offered.

The purpose of this training is to instill a strong and secure self-confidence in the use of energetics in daily activities. Muscle-response testing skills will be taught so each student attains a high aptitude from which to verify intuitive insights.

The mission of this work is to enhance awarenesses, intuition, communications, actions, ethical parameters and concentration.

This Fundamentals of Body Energetics Training Course is not designed to teach any extraordinary healing techniques. By understanding more about the nature of body energetics, your conscious thoughts will reflect your personal, ethical, logical and intuitive perspectives. This translates gracefully into every action which you undertake. Since your perspectives define your attitudes, your philosophy of life and your memories will be dictated from your attitudes. These attitudes will enhance your evolution.

With this training you will gain skills to:
• Discern the energetic characteristics of situations.
• Determine and understand the emotional attitudes that obscure solutions that could remove the undesirable condition.
• Pinpoint how resistances that may stem from fear or imagined detrimental consequences are aggravating any present conflict.
• Using your pure motivation and pure desire, discover the particular vulnerable areas where you protect yourself against imagined harm.

Sue Gurnee will post the descriptions of each of the upcoming Training Courses on her website - **www.suegurnee.com**

APPENDIX

At Growing Wheel we have assembled an eclectic collection of items useful for interns.

Living in a virtually unspoiled environment surrounded by thousands of trees, some interns begin a detoxification process. When they tune into their body's needs, they begin searching for ways to hasten the optimal functioning of their systems.

Therapies to enhance health
- Diet regime
- Hypnotherapy
- Aromatherapy
- Ionization Therapy
- Gemstone Therapy
- Sacred Sound Therapy
- Iridology
- Silent Retreat
- Color Therapy with Dinhshaw Color Gels
- Flower Essence Remedies
- Meditation

Bodywork
- Progressive Muscle Relaxation
- Pilates Method of Balancing
- Yoga
- Rolfing
- Reflexology
- T'ai Chi
- Cranial-Sacral Therapy
- Feldenkrais Technique
- Shiatsu/Acupressure
- Alexander Technique
- Massage
- Structural Integration

Additional Personal Care
- Hydrotherapy
- Herbal Preparations
- Allopathic Procedures
- Acupuncture
- Dentistry
- Homeopathy

Self Care

It is essential that your vitamins, minerals, and other health-giving components of food adequately supply you with the power needed to be of service to yourself and others. You may deplete your amino acids, vitamins, minerals, and enzymes through stress and by ignoring your nutritional needs.

How is your body's micro-nutrition?

APPENDIX

Use a scale 1-100. (Your sustained goal is 100.)

Check, using muscle-response testing, if these essential and non-essential amino acids are functioning and synthesizing the proteins essential for your personal health.

There are 20 amino acids that form the building blocks of all proteins. These amino acids are necessary for the formation of neurotransmitters in the brain.

There are eight essential amino acids:
• Phenylalanine
• Valine
• Threonine
• Tryptophan
• Isoleucine
• Methionine
• Lysine
• Leucine

There are twelve "non-essential" amino acids; that can be produced by the body:
• Arginine
• Aspartic Acid
• Cysteine
• Glutamine
• Glycine
• Histadine
• Alanine
• Methionine
• Phenylalanine
• Proline
• Tyrosine
• Serine

Growing Wheel's Self Care Kit

Homeopathy sees symptoms as a positive outward sign that the body is trying to balance itself. Any symptom you recognize within yourself is a reflection of your current movement toward regaining health. Since you are not prescribing these for others, I feel it is appropriate to muscle test and ask your own body what it may need. This opens your insights and widens awarenesses about further areas to place personal attention.

Homeopathy:

As a general rule, low potencies (like 6c) are used for chronic conditions and higher potencies (like 30c) are for acute conditions, such as a cold. Remedies for acute conditions are usually taken on a half-hourly basis at first and then the intervals spread out to about 8-12 hours. More chronic conditions may combine both low and high potencies. Since this energy medicine treats the whole, it addresses your physical, mental and emotional parts.

I suggest that you take only one remedy at a time and remember not to touch the remedies with your fingers. Empty one tiny white pellet onto a teaspoon and put the remedy under your tongue. Take remedies at least 30 minutes after a meal so your mouth is "clean" of other vibrations. Avoid spicy or minty foods or beverages that may antidote remedies. Store the tightly closed bottles in a cool dark area away from strong smells such as perfumes or essential oils. Homeopathic remedies, if protected, keep their potency for about 5 years.

Growing Wheel's Homeopathy kit that is kept on hand:

- Aconite: compounded fears, fear of death
- Aethusa cynapium: thoughtless or imprudent behavior
- Aslepias tuberosa: weak sense of self
- Arsenicum album: poisoning (on any dimension)
- Causticum: ailments from injustice
- Cocculus: ailments from lack of sleep; useful for those who nurse the sick
- Coffea: excitability, mental over stimulation, sleeplessness
- Fluoricum acidum: burn-out remedy
- Kali phosphoricum: ear noises from nervous exhaustion; want of nerve power
- Nux vomica: travel sickness, digestive problems, nausea and headache
- Ozone: ultimate burn-out remedy
- Palladium metallicum: seeks positive opinion of others, keeps brightly in company but much exhausted later
- Ruta: for eye strain
- Sulphur: difficulty remembering words and names; fear of not reaching one's goals
- Thuja: manipulative, no completion, no point
- Ignatia: sensitivity to tobacco smoke

Our Summer Kit *Caring For Yourself* includes homeopathic remedies for:
- Indigestion
- Nervousness
- Insomnia
- Exhaustion
- Insect Bites
- Injuries
- Swelling and Inflammation

• Headache
• Lack of Energy

Near the end of the 19th century, a German physician, Wilhelm Schuessler experimented and later developed 12 vital tissue salts that are a homeopathically prepared combination of minerals.

These are available in health stores with the following names:
• CALC. PHOS. produced from calcium phosphate
• CALC. SULF. produced from calcium sulfate
• FERR. PHOS. produced from iron phosphate
• SIL. produced from silicon dioxide
• KALI MUR. produced from potassium chloride
• KALI PHOS. produced from potassium phosphate
• KALI SULF. produced from potassium sulfate
• MAG. PHOS. produced from magnesium phosphate
• CALC. FLUOR. produced from calcium fluoride
• NAT. MUR. produced from sodium chloride
• NAT. PHOS. produced from sodium phosphate
• NAT. SULF. produced from sodium sulfate

Dowse the above list. Are you depleted in any of these 12 areas?

Essential oils that assist in eliminating stress include rosemary, ginger, and lemongrass.

Many interns have benefited from vocabulary words to help them identify their feelings.

LIST OF DISCORDANT WORDS

abnormal

abused

afraid

aggravated

ambivalent

annoyed

antagonistic

anxious

apathetic

argumentative

arrogant

attacked

barren

belligerent

betrayed

bitchy

bossy

burdened

castrated

clumsy

compulsive

contrary

cowardly

defiant

delusional

destructive

devious

disengaged

dissatisfied

distraught

ditched

drained

empty

entangled

erratic

evasive

exaggerated

exploited

fanatical

fearful

flat

forceful

frazzled

frustrated

furious

hostile

ignored

inconsiderate

indulgent

ineffectual

inferior

inflexible

intimidated

intolerant

irresponsible

irritable

irritated

irritated

jealous

lazy

locked-in

lonesome

manipulated

miffed

miserly

mournful

nagged

narcissistic

neurotic

numb

obsessive

opinionated

overburdened

paranoid

persecuted

pessimistic

pious

rebellious

reckless

resistant

rigid

rude

separate

silly

sinful

spineless

stern

stiff

stubborn

stuck

submissive

subversive

thwarted

trapped

unacknowledged

underdeveloped

undeserving

unstable

used

vague

vengeful

violated

violent

worthless

54 POSITIVE TRAITS TO CULTIVATE:

Acceptance

Adaptability

Admirability

Altruism

Ambition

Appreciation

Commitment

Compassion

Comprehension

Conscientiousness

Cooperation

Courage

Creativity

Decisiveness

Dedication

Emotional honesty

Empathy

Entusiasm

Equanimity

Faithfulness

Generosity

Gratitude

Individuality

Insight

Involvement

Joyousness

Kindness

Knowledge

Loyalty

Magnanimity

Mastery

Objectivity

Originality

Patience

Practicality

Productivity

Receptivity

Reliability

Resilience

Reasonableness

Self-assurance

Self-awareness

Self-confidence

Self-development

Self-discipline

Self-esteem

Self-possession

Self-reliance

Sensibility

Tolerance

Understanding

Unself-consciousness

Unselfishness

Wisdom

INTERNS WRITE...

By the Gate House is a box for comments. Here is what we found in the box at the end of the program last year.

Comment 1

When I saw the gravel roads around the property I want to go home. My car was not going up the driveway. I complained and Sue made a swft comment that I could park by mailboxes and walk to the deck. She was wearink clothes that did not make her look like a teachr. A big St. Bernard-like dog lay by her site so I could not sit next to her. She dint squint in the full sunlight and dint sweat. She drank no water and dint make any mistakes in her speech. I don't like her. She upsets me because she is so perfect. I can't figure out how old she is and her hair always looks good. She only wears earrings and no other jewelry. I don't know if she is married. She travels a lot so maybe has lovers all over the world. I think she likes me but she has not talkt to me at lunch when she makes the rounds to each table. Does she know that I am afraid of her? Tomorrow I will let her no about the pain in my lower back.

Comment 2

There is no way to describe the wonderment I feel in this setting. I am alive for the first time in my life. Sue Gurnee is such a band leader. I want to play every instrument I have inside. She is the most honest and authentic person I have ever met. I saw her in many difficult situations. I was happy that she could show her emotions in a way that let others know that she had boundaries that could not be crossed. She is also the most tolerant person I have ever seen!! Growing Wheel is a haven and I think Sue is an angel.

Comment 3

I am sad to leave and want to go to Oakview one more time to listen to the birds and bugs. How lucky I am to be here and learn.

In the Gate House mailbox:

Letter 1

Dear Sue,

I have been home for 2 weeks since in Todd. It is uncanny. My husband and children have changed completely. I can't say how. It is just that we are laughing more. Working together as a team and even are making plans to go on a vacation to Martha's Vineyard to see friends. Our family feels so cohesive. I am shocked. I didn't do anything!!! I send you love and gratitude.

Blessings.

Letter 2

Dear Sue,

I am writing from a clinic in India where I have worked for the past 2 years. After spending the summer with you, I decided to become a nurse. It was a surprise to my family. My mother said that I probably would not be able to graduate or get a job. I followed my authentic desires and passed all the requirements with highest grades. Within a few weeks I was offered a job and then, well, here I am. Fulfilling my dreams. I send you my gratitude and appreciation. You gave me the tools I needed. You are the best!

A RECENT INTERN
ABOUT INÉE ADER

Inée May Alta Ader was born in Haifa, Israel in 1989 and grew up in Santa Fe, New Mexico from the age of three. From there, she developed into quite the spunky and precocious 23-year-old girl she is today. She is a loving adherent to the Baha'i Faith—an independent religion emerging in 1844 whose basic principles are the unity of all humankind, Progressive Revelation, and the equality of men and women. Her life ambition is to become a Naturopathic doctor and open her own creative practice of a Universal Center for Alternative Healthcare and Naturopathic Medicine. Inée is particularly fond of science fiction and fantasy novels, being a vegetarian/ borderline vegan, eating and preparing delicious whole foods for healing, and very bad weather. In between school work and various volunteer initiatives, she loves painting and drawing, to participate in group acro-yoga and acro-balance workshops, playing the Navajo Flute, Didgeridoo, and guitar, hiking in the mountains, and nesting quietly with snacks and a movie. Inée is an inquisitive young lady with an almost foolish optimism, which she tries to infect everyone with.

A RECENT INTERN

Because there are no grades, diplomas, or prizes given to any intern after his or her summer study at Growing Wheel, but for those who have truly earned it, we have developed a policy of giving letters of recommendation.

Here is Growing Wheel's Open Letter of Recommendation for Inée.

To whom it may concern,

There are five branches on the special love of wisdom tree that is called in Greek — Philosophy. These five branches — metaphysics, epistemology, logic, ethics and aesthetics are not often a source of interest to many people in their early 20's. Philosophers often rally around these five historically modeled branches and languidly swing in the shade of the well-documented knowledge. Intuition and the power of energetics naturally sprout from the tree's healthy branches. They too are part of the nature of reality. Answers to the questions that are considered metaphysics, create deep patterns of clarity that are willingly being taught along side those versed in the hard sciences.

I am proud that you, Inée, are interested in pursuing a health-related career as a Naturopath. Your short apprenticeship was a hard training during some chapters at the Growing Wheel campus. Your internship, from my perspective will serve you in all future encounters.

Emergency situations that you will undoubtedly be confronted with will not frighten you. You will use training from Growing Wheel to think quickly and react efficiently. In areas where you must maintain your integrity when others may not find this important, you can call upon your well-established strong discipline bound by your faith. This will serve you well.

168

A RECENT INTERN

Your inquisitiveness and genuine interest in people is a magic formula you have learned well. Keep up the genuine interest in the power of food and continue to lavish delicious meals on those who understand the power of food for health. Kudos for the well thought out and elegantly presented Inée-salads that quietly and with pluck floated from kitchen to table. I would recommend you to anyone as a very special candidate for future projects that require the talents and dedication you possess.

Sincerely,

Susan Gurnee

GROWING WHEEL DIRECTOR
ABOUT SUE GURNEE

Susan Gurnee is the founder and director of Growing Wheel International Inc., in the wilds of North Carolina. Its mission is to promote awareness and conscious communication with people and the environment through advanced creative endeavors.

Sue wears multidimensional hats. She is an artist, a healer, and a teacher of health care professionals in the USA and abroad. Her resume also includes that she graduated from wilderness survival school at 15 to later become a park ranger at Bear Mountain State Park in New York and segued into working as a guide/counselor at an outdoor awareness camp in the Catskills. Oh, that was after she recorded educational records for ten years with Silver Burdett for the series "Making Music Your Own" for US public schools before attending Drew University.

After college, at age 20 she led teenagers from the lower-east side of Manhattan on canoe trips through the Adirondacks following the route made famous by Thoreau. After receiving her master's degree in trompe l'oeil painting she painted Resonance art mural commissions for private homes in New York and California and followed the wildebeest migration each winter as she co-led adventure-awareness safaris to East Africa.

She founded Brickside Studio, an exhibit design and fabrication company. There her team recreated habitats (dioramas) for permanent exhibits in zoos and museums around the USA. Her work can be seen at the JungleWorld exhibit at the Bronx Zoo, the Oakland Museum, the Newark Museum, and the New York City Jewish Museum. In the movie industry she became a union scenic artist (Local 829) and had the pleasure of sharing her artistic as well as healing skills with many talented actors and crewmembers.

After following a higher directive she moved from the beach side movie-making town of Wilmington, North Carolina to a forest retreat in the Appalachian Mountains. There she began a complex experiment within nature. She worked fervently to preserve a pristine expanse of natural beauty along one of the oldest rivers in the world.

On a hundred acres of forest that had seen only two previous owners since the 1800's, with a small group of talented artisans, Sue fashioned her special hand-built home where she has spent the past years in co-creative alliance, utilizing the energetics of nature for mutual benefits.

She continues to write books and paint. Each year she exhibits her artwork in New York, Berlin, and Zurich. She fulfills commissions for her Resonance Art that holds a vibration that enhances well-being.

Time in the woods gave her practical understanding of the Universal Principles. The visitors, students and interns who have wandered to her estate from Holland, United States, Germany, Switzerland, Italy, and other parts of the globe have learned firsthand that all things are interconnected and nothing goes unnoticed in the Universal Order of things.

When asked, Sue reflects that the time spent in devoted independent study of the language of energetics was invaluable training. "Nature is always providing a leaping off place to pluck the multidimensional secrets that lie within reach."

Her depth and breadth of proficiency are formidable. Her style is witty, honest and exuberant. To know her is a treasure that sparkles in every moment.

CONTACT INFORMATION

suegurnee@growingwheel.com

www.fieldsofunderstanding.com
www.suegurnee.com
www.growingwheel.com
www.diamondgardening.org

For private consultations with
Sue Gurnee call:

828.262.0011

Hours to make
half-hour phone appointments:
Tuesdays, Wednesdays, and Thursdays
from 9am to 9:30am New York time.

Tax-exempt donations
can be made by check to:
Growing Wheel International Inc.
and mailed to:

PO Box 5
Todd, NC, 28684
USA